Young
2004 POETRY

GW00599275

ONCE UPON A RHYME

IMAGINATION FOR A NEW GENERATION

Co Antrim Vol II

Edited by Natalie Catterick

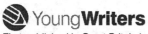 Young**Writers**

First published in Great Britain in 2004 by:
Young Writers
Remus House
Coltsfoot Drive
Peterborough
PE2 9JX
Telephone: 01733 890066
Website: www.youngwriters.co.uk

SB ISBN 1 84460 529 9

Foreword

Young Writers was established in 1991 and has been passionately devoted to the promotion of reading and writing in children and young adults ever since. The quest continues today. Young Writers remains as committed to engendering the fostering of burgeoning poetic and literary talent as ever.

This year's Young Writers competition has proven as vibrant and dynamic as ever and we are delighted to present a showcase of the best poetry from across the UK. Each poem has been carefully selected from a wealth of *Once Upon A Rhyme* entries before ultimately being published in this, our twelfth primary school poetry series.

Once again, we have been supremely impressed by the overall high quality of the entries we have received. The imagination, energy and creativity which has gone into each young writer's entry made choosing the best poems a challenging and often difficult but ultimately hugely rewarding task - the general high standard of the work submitted amply vindicating this opportunity to bring their poetry to a larger appreciative audience.

We sincerely hope you are pleased with our final selection and that you will enjoy *Once Upon A Rhyme Co Antrim Vol II* for many years to come.

Contents

Kerry Thompson (10)	21
Adam McAllister (10)	21
Jack McWilliams (9)	22
Matthew Whittley (9)	22
Melissa Boyd (9)	23
Lauren Lavery (9)	23
Elaine Uprichard (9)	24
Phillip Henderson (9)	24
Zara Morrow (10)	25
Ben Robinson (10)	25
Stefan Mullen (9)	25
Anne Sheridan (10)	26
Christine Rea (10)	27
Hannah Sullivan (10)	27
Bethany Doig (10)	28
Rachael Lowry (9)	28
Garry Tilbury (9)	29
Lindsey Kerr (10)	29
Jordan Bustard (10)	30
Fiona Brown (10)	30
Nicole Millar (9)	31
Ian Hamill (10)	31
Lucianna Hughes (9)	32
Sian Allen (10)	32
Lindsay Meaklim (10)	33
Elizabeth Glenfield (9)	33
Jordan Quinn (8)	33
Shannon Peoples (8)	34
Julia Coulter (9)	34

Ballygolan Primary School

Rebecca Caldwell (8)	34
Thomas McKee (8)	35
Rachel Cochrane (8)	35
Craig Graham (8)	35
Samuel Waite (8)	36
Jamie Kirkpatrick (9)	36
Andrew McGovern (8)	36
Rebecca Boland (9)	37

Ballymoney Model Primary School

Michael Thompson (11)	37
Tiffany Gage (10)	38
Jamie Forsythe (8)	38
Steven McDonald (10)	39
Lucy Maxwell (11)	39
Gemma Linton (11)	40
Mark Coulter (10)	41
David Thompson (10)	41
Brad McClenaghan (11)	42
Judith Kelly (10)	42
Siobhan Brown (10)	43
Jordan Connelly (11)	43
Yasmin Walker (11)	44
Alan Gordon (10)	44
Andrew Hanna (10)	45
Rachael Martin (10)	45
John Doherty (11)	46
Jonny Kinnaird (9)	46
Aaron Lamont (10)	47
Rebekah Knight (11)	47
Linzi Watton (9)	47
Laura Witherow (10)	48
Andrew Mills (10)	48
Shiona Rankin (10)	49
Jade McElderry (11)	49
Nikki Boreland (9)	49
Christopher Cunningham (11)	50
Olivia Pethick (10)	50
Charlotte Ross (10)	51
Mark Crooks (10)	51
Darren Rennie (11)	52
Meghan Christie (10)	52
Mark Lyons (10)	53
Kelli Morrison (10)	53
Emma Ferris (10)	54
Sarah Dempster (10)	55
Rachel McElfatrick (10)	55
Jade Watton (9)	55
Gemma Glendinning (10)	56
David Barkley (10)	56

Paige Walker (10)	56
Terri Kelly (10)	57
Chantelle Caulfield (9)	57
Victoria McGregor (9)	57
Dean Clayton (10)	58
Simon McKendry (9)	58
Laura McIlveen (9)	58
Gemma Fox (10)	59
Thomas Knight (9)	60
Nicola McCollum (9)	60
Dillon Connelly (9)	60
Albany Ferguson-Smith (9)	61
Aaron McKendry (9)	61
Ricki Stewart (9)	61
Jonathan Tweed (8)	62
Jenna-Leah Lynch (8)	62
Philip Linton (9)	62
Charis Wilson (9)	63
Hannah McKinney (8)	63
Johnny Allan (9)	64
Bethany Millican (9)	64
Lauren McIroy (8)	65
Ryan Sweetman (9)	65
Priyanka Kher (9)	65
Paige McClements (9)	66
Danielle Gordon (8)	66
Scott Anderson (8)	67
Danny White (9)	67
Danielle Stewart (9)	68
David Stirling (8)	68
Jimmy Mariano (7)	68
Peter Johnston (9)	69
Lucy McWilliams (9)	69
Hannah Witherow (8)	69
Amber-Rose McIntyre (9)	70
Naomi Connelly (9)	70
Lesley-Anne Hanna (9)	71
Ross Jackson (8)	72
Sarah-Louise Leighton (8)	72
Emma Chen (7)	72
Amy McMullan (8)	73
Peter Wilson (7)	73

Daniel Christie (7)	74
Gillian Henry (8)	74
Jolene McKinney (8)	74
Khara Rennie (8)	75
Jamie Hanna (8)	75
Tristan Fox (8)	75
Megan McWilliams (8)	76
Chloe Kelly (8)	76
David McGoldrick (8)	77
Ryan Ennis (8)	77
Allister Anderson (8)	78
Hannah Graham (7)	78
Parisa Robinson (8)	78
Timothy Woods (8)	79
John Coulter (8)	79
Thomas Pethick (8)	79
Roger Gage (8)	80
Megann Crawford (7)	80
Abbey Boreland (7)	80
Cara McConville (7)	81
Niamh Rankin (7)	81
Shannon Holmes (8)	82
Jodie Wilson (7)	82
Alexs Hutchinson (7)	82
Robert Smyth (8)	83
Kirbie McClenaghan (8)	83
Olivia McConaghie (8)	83

Brownlee Primary School

Victoria Price (11)	84
James Magee (9)	84
Tara Townsley (10)	85
Lauren Mason (11)	85
Natalie Bresland (11)	86
Nicole Machray (10)	86

Carr Primary School

Victoria Mayers (11)	87
Kristopher Wilson (10)	87
Robert McGibbon (8)	88
Matthew Stewart (10)	88

Claire Windrum (7)	88
Matthew Stewart (10)	89
Heather Earney (9)	89
Andrew Mills (8)	90

Carryduff Primary School

Jonathan English (10)	90
Lee Waring (11)	90
Lee Graham (11)	91
Richard Bradfield (11)	91
Anna Marshall (11)	92
Sarah Gowen (10)	92
Abigail Magowan (11) & Charlotte McCune (11)	93
Mark Carson (10)	93
Lauren Hall (11)	94
Jamie Patterson (11)	94
Emma Payne (11)	95
Darren Lawthers (11)	95
Zoe Harron (11)	96

Harmony Hill Primary School

Susan Hunter (10)	96
Rachel McCulla (10)	97
Michelle Roberts (10)	97
Ben Johnson (10)	98
Joshua Porter (8)	98
Paula McCalmont (10)	99
Shannon Rea (10)	99
Stewart Gavin (10)	100
Christopher Moore (10)	100
Emily Smith (10)	101
Carrie-Ann Brady (10)	101
Nathan Adams (9)	102
Rebekah Leathem (9)	102
Rachel McGrath (8)	102
Christopher Ferguson (9)	103
Nicole Brown (8)	103
Ross Walker (9)	103
Marcus Sedman (9)	104
Anna Jones (10)	104
Siân Porter (9)	105

Andrew McStea (9)	105
Alicia Whitworth (9)	106
Natalie Nicol (10)	106
Rachel Devenney (10)	107
Sam Coates (9)	107
Olivia Wilson (10)	108
Sophia Reynor (8)	108
Megan Herdman (9)	109
Jessica McKnight (8)	109
Amy Hamilton (9)	109
Nicola Annett (9)	110
Stuart Wilson (9)	110
Danielle Agnew (9)	110
James Dowse (8)	111
Ashleigh Patterson (9)	111

Linn Primary School

Thomas Smyth (9)	111
Hayleigh Brereton (11)	112
Louise Wylie (11)	112
Alice Cameron (11)	113
Aimée Agnew (11)	113
Tracey Todd (11)	114
Ryan Campbell (10)	114
Victoria McFetridge (11)	115
Zoe Zolene Mayberry (10)	115
Patricia Leitch (11)	116
Scott McClelland (9)	116
Hannah McKay (10)	117
Grace Clements (10)	117
Carolyn Robinson (11)	118
Heather Preshaw (10)	118
Kim Hamilton (10)	119
David Murray (10)	119
Brandon Wilson (10)	120

Portrush Primary School

Shelley Barclay (9)	120
Scott Graham (10)	121
Aaron Kane (11)	122
Amber Callaghan (10)	122

Kathryn Bawn (11)	138
Kathryn Edwards (11)	138
Peter McAlernon (11)	139
Thomas Wallace Bigger (11)	139
Heather Mallon (10)	140
Suzi Ernst (11)	140

St Joseph's Primary School, Dunloy

Ciaran McIlfatrick (9)	140
Conor Crawford (10)	141
Ronan Cunning (9)	141
Justin Drain (11)	142
Lauren Elliott (10)	142
Rosie McNamee (9)	142
Niall O'Boyle (11)	143
Seamus McLaughlin (11)	143
Katherine McToal (11)	143
Emma Dooey (11)	144
Melissa Cunning (11)	144
Paul Cochrane (9)	145
Patsy Martin (10)	145
Ronan Shivers (9)	145
Thomas McCann (9)	146
Patrick Magee (9)	146
Lauren McQuillan (8)	147
John-lee Smyth (9)	147
Niall Doherty (8)	148
Aimee McPoland (9)	148
Christy Drain (9)	149
Caoimhe McCullagh (9)	149
Adam O'Kane (9)	150
James Kearns (8)	150
Sean Hurl (9)	151
Olivia McLaughlin (9)	151
Ryan Reynolds (9)	152
Nichola Cassidy (9)	152
Sorcha Doherty (8)	153
Daren Cunning (9)	153
James McFall (8)	154
Kevin Armstrong (8)	154
Niamh McAuley (9)	155

The Poems

Seasons

Seasons, seasons
Bright, dull and in-between
Winter is the coldest
And just plain mean.

Summer, brighter days
Sun is rising high
Hardly any clouds
In the bright blue sky.

In spring, flowers are growing
Birds lay their eggs
Hibernating animals
Stretch their wakening legs.

Autumn leaves
Fall off trees
Oh, what a mystery
Mother Nature weaves.

Lauren Greene (10)
Abbots Cross Primary School

Rainforest

The rainforest, the rainforest, it's never asleep
Even through the night when you don't hear a peep
The tiger's searching for its prey
And making the green grass sway.

When all the animals wake up and yawn
The tropical birds sing their morning song
They're all flying through the skies
It's lovely! It's amazing! It's such a prize.

The monkeys that swing through the trees
Are all enjoying the forest breeze
Their little babies smile with glee
Because they're happy, wild and free.

Carly Gilmore (11)
Abbots Cross Primary School

Summer Days

S ummer days are so much fun
U nderwater in the sun
M y body is so red
M ummy, I'm getting sunburn!
E very day I go out to play
R unning round the garden.

D on't need to go to school - no work!
A lways licking lollies
Y es, it is so much fun
S unbathing in the garden.

Jordan Woolley (9)
Ashgrove Primary School

School

School, oh school, sitting in class,
Daydreaming - got notes to pass!
Having fun in the playground with my friends,
Bells ring, playtime ends.

It's ten to three,
School's over, yippee!

Sophie Waters (9)
Ashgrove Primary School

Rugby

Rugby is good and rugby is fun,
It can be hard,
Rugby is wonderful,
But it can be a big game,
It's my dream to play for Ulster.

Paul Kyle (8)
Ashgrove Primary School

Football

F ootball, oh mighty football, I love you so
O h, so much fun
O h, so great
T ricking other players
B all's in the net
A ll the goals are mine
L ife would be miserable without football
L ife is good because football's here!

Jonathan Torrens (9)
Ashgrove Primary School

My Favourite Pet

My favourite pet is fluffy and scruffy,
It jumps round the field in the midday light,
It's so cute and soft,
It feels like a little pillow,
It runs over hills
And jumps and jumps away.

Emma Whitten (8)
Ashgrove Primary School

My Favourite Place

My favourite place is not outer space,
My favourite place is not Rome,
It's warm and comfy,
And it's called home.

Jennifer Thompson (9)
Ashgrove Primary School

Saturday Morning

Saturday morning, it's eight o'clock
Don't want to listen to my alarm clock
Everyone's up, my mum's coming in
My brother woke me with a big, smiley grin
I just want to sleep for an hour or two
But cartoons are on telly
I got up - wouldn't you?

Shannen McClenaghan (9)
Ashgrove Primary School

Kind And Generous

Come here, gather round,
Me and my family won a thousand pounds.
Me and my dad got a bit mad,
But give me a break, I'm a little lad.
Then there was another war,
So we decided to help the poor.

Jonathan Carlisle (9)
Ashgrove Primary School

Friends

Friends are very funny and they are such fun.
It's really fun playing with my best friends.
In my friend's garden we tell funny jokes.
Nearly every day we play with each other.
Desperate to play football together out in the sun.
Sunny days we play out on the lovely green grass
playing . . . football!

Rayhaan Ali (9)
Ashgrove Primary School

Football

F riends and I watch a match
O h, the referee points to the spot
O n the pitch is the best player
T he penalty has been missed
B e a sport and pass the ball
A lways play fairly on the pitch
L inesmen aren't being fair
L ate winner for our team.

Jamie Moore (9)
Ashgrove Primary School

Animals

A is for amazing, special and cute
N is for noisy, you wish they could be mute
I is for irresistible, cuddly and dreamy
M is for magical and ultra weenie
A is for adorable and nippy teeth
L is for lovely, like a floral wreath
S is simply the best - *animals!*

Chloe Hume (11)
Ashgrove Primary School

My Space Adventure

S pace is so cool
P eople think it is not real
A stronauts visit all the time
C reepy things float around
E verything's cool up here
  I wish I could come again.

Hannah McMillan (9)
Ashgrove Primary School

My Teacher

M y teacher can shout sometimes
Y ou'll always get help if you're stuck

T eachers are bossy, mine's sometimes like that
E ach pupil's work she marks
A nd when you fall or it's your birthday, she'll give you a sticker
C ool and kind, that's my teacher
H ow she is always nice
E very now and then she spots someone talking
R ight, ten lines!
   I'm sorry miss
   That's OK she'd say.

Lydia Startin (9)
Ashgrove Primary School

My Birthday Party

Today's my party,
I can't wait,
The doorbell's ringing,
My friends are here,
The disco's on,
Ohh party, party on.

Amy-Leigh Trimble (9)
Ashgrove Primary School

Snow

S now, snow, falling on the ground
N o one to be found
O nly a snowman standing still
W aiting at the top of the hill.

Ellen McCartney (9)
Ashgrove Primary School

The Rickety Fence

The rickety fence
The rickety fence
Give it a pick it's
The pickety fence,
Give it a lick it's
A lickety fence,
Give it a click it's
A clickety fence.
Give it a pick
Give it a lick
Give it a click
With a rickety stick!
Rickety
Pickety
Clickety
Click!

Katie Luney (7)
Ashgrove Primary School

My Friend, Debra

My friend, Debra, is very kind
She is the sort that would cross your mind
About fun and giggles.

My friend, Debra, is a milly,
She sometimes is a silly billy,
She has brown hair and brown eyes.

She has a small nose and a big smile,
She has hairspray and I must say,
She can't live without it.

Jessica Molyneaux (9)
Ashgrove Primary School

12 Months Of 2004

January comes at the start of the year,
It's very cold where we live here!

February comes, it's Valentine's time,
People send cards, which usually rhyme.

March begins the new season - spring,
And lots of birds come out to sing!

April is the month with Easter Day,
When we get off for a week from school, hooray!

May comes with two birthdays,
My mum's and mine - hip, hip, hooray!

My dad's birthday comes in June,
We'll get his name on a special balloon!

Our summer holidays are in July,
When to the school we say a final goodbye!

August is usually very hot,
That's when we get to play a lot!

September brings us new school woes,
Along with that some new school clothes!

October ends with Hallowe'en,
To go and see fireworks, we're very keen!

November holds the dreaded 11-plus,
Thank goodness that's all over for us!

December finishes up the year,
With lots of yuletide fun and cheer!

Ben Newell (10)
Ashgrove Primary School

12 Months Of The Year

January starts on New Year's Day,
Then come the Xmas debts to pay!

February comes, it's Valentine's Day,
Expressing love in a rhyming way.

March brings work the whole way through,
Maths, English and science too.

April has little showers of rain,
And then hay fever starts again.

In May the children dance around,
The giant maypole in the ground.

June brings the first rays of sun,
This means the summer has just begun.

July is hot, make no mistake,
Now we need a well-earned break.

August sun still smiles on you,
Time to plan a barbecue.

September starts secondary education,
As well as extra concentration.

October, the time of Hallowe'en,
I see witches, monsters and a beautiful queen.

November has a coloured sky,
Because of the fireworks sent up high.

December, the time to celebrate,
The Christmas holiday feels so great.

Ryan Cochrane (11)
Ashgrove Primary School

The Months

January is the month of winds and frost,
And so we celebrate my brother's birth.

And February is the end of winter,
When we will get our 11-plus results.

March is the month with rain and sun,
This makes flowers spring and grow.

April is the month with Easter,
Which gives us eggs and also showers.

And May is the end of warm, calm spring,
With lambs and chicks and blooming flowers.

June is the start of summer,
So we P7s leave Ashgrove forever.

July is the hottest month of the year,
So I celebrate my birthday and holiday.

August is the end of summer,
With summer rain to keep us cool.

September is the start of autumn,
And also the start of a new school.

October is cold and frosty,
Leaves are falling and it's Hallowe'en time.

November is the end of autumn,
All the trees are dull and bare.

December is the start of another cold winter,
And the children are excited about Christmas.

Simon Gibson (11)
Ashgrove Primary School

The Months

January comes, we're back at school,
Hooray, we're off to a party.

February's here, results appear,
Great, we're going to my cousins.

Fun March, brother's birthday arrives,
We're off to another party.

Joyful April, there's eggs to eat,
While rested nice and warm asleep.

Restful May, it's Bank Holiday,
Having fun at the May Day fair.

June comes back at boring old school,
While some are off in lovely warm bed.

Noisy July as the bands walk by,
Glorious colours with the flags high.

August brings the wheat and barley,
And gives us plenty to eat.

Exciting September, gifts appear,
It's my birthday, give a cheer.

October brings fun and fireworks,
Hallowe'en masks and witches' black cats.

Bare November, leaves on the ground,
Little bits of snowflakes all around.

Chilly December, real cold outside,
Getting near to Christmas, white around.

Rebecca McRoberts (11)
Ashgrove Primary School

The Year

January   Back to school,
            Hope this is cool.

February   When the letter goes through the door,
            Now I know the transfer test results are here.

March   Brings breezes and light winds,
            Plus stirs the dancing daffodils.

April   Easter eggs with lovely bows,
            Makes children's faces glow.

May   Dance and sing at the fair,
            Lovely honeycomb, I'll be there.

June   Finish school, hip, hip, hooray,
            Only just another day.

July   There is the bonfire and the bands,
            The Union Jack in people's hands.

August   On our way on the plane,
            Somewhere nice, let's say Spain.

September   Back to school once again,
            Now with work, what a pain.

October   The leaves turn brown and start to fall,
            Brown conkers for us all.

November   This month brings the transfer test,
            We all work hard and do our best.

December   Christmas comes, my birthday too,
            Lots of presents just for you.

Ben Fletcher (11)
Ashgrove Primary School

The Months

January and I'm back to school
I've had too much turkey and I'm more than full.

It's February, my results are out
If I get an 'A' I'll scream and shout.

It's *go, go, go!* 'Cause we're in March
And this is where the F1 season starts.

April Fool's Day is such fun
Just make sure you're not the stupid one.

It's May and the lambs are prancing to and fro
Look, there's a fox, stone the crows!

June's well cool 'cause
We're off school.

It's July and the holidays they come, they creep
I'm so excited I can hardly sleep.

It's August, oh mercy, how can it be?
Because that means there's only one month left of the
school holiday.

It's September already, a new school for me
Oh crumbs! Oh help! Oh mercy be!

It's October and I'm one month in
The school dinners are disgusting and I'm rather thin.

On to November, only one month to go
But now it's my birthday, where I'll get lots of dough!

At last it's December, almost a new year
Some people will celebrate with a bit of beer.

Matthew Robinson (11)
Ashgrove Primary School

Months Of The Year Poem

January, taking the short walk to school,
In the winter snow so cool

February began with a good old cheer,
As my birthday grew so near

March, all I ever did was play with my games,
I wish it was June for school to end

April, I was longing for my Easter eggs,
Not to mention the week off school

May, I moved house, just a quick reminder,
School is almost over for this term

June, school's out for summer,
Hip, hip, hurrah

July, Dad's off work now,
We all can go on holiday

August holidays are nearly over,
Now new uniforms for next term

September, back to school,
Boo hoo hoo

October, mid-term break is near,
It's time to trick or treat and watch the fireworks

November, the 11-plus exam has come,
Although I'm not sitting it

December has just passed
My brother's birthday at the start
Jesus' birthday near the end, presents I got.

Christopher Pattison (11)
Ashgrove Primary School

The Months

January the month of snow
Back to school the children go

February the snow is thawing
Not long left before it's gone

March is often cold and breezy
Many people end up sneezy

April can be rather cool
So stay nice and warm, don't be an April fool

May is warming up a bit
Though you can barely notice it

June is when sheep lose their wool
Kids are getting out of school

July's the month when people say
'I think I'd like a holiday'

August's very warm and sunny
But wasps and bees are not funny

September can be very cruel
For the kids return to school

October's getting rather chilly
So wrap up warm and don't be silly

November can be cold and grey
The wind blows all the leaves away

December is a month of greed
When people like to feed and feed.

Andrew Robinson (11)
Ashgrove Primary School

My Dream School

In my school I'd like a pool
To start the day, refreshingly cool
You'd wear ordinary clothes
To strike a big pose
And when the teachers decided to mark
The children could have fun at the park
In the playground
There'd be a harmonious sound
Some would kick ball
And no one would ever get injured or fall
Teachers could drink steaming coffee
As long as we got to chew toffee
And at the end of the day when the bell would ring
The children would still be happy enough to sing.

Hannah McKinstry (9)
Ashgrove Primary School

The Months

January, new year, parties all night, more snow!
February, cold and bitter, workmen out with the gritter.
March, spring has sprung, flowers are blooming.
April, the rainy showers, the pretty flowers all in bloom.
May, all the baby animals, cute and sweet, walking for the
                                        first time on their feet.
June, the longest day, the hot weather coming.
July, holidays hooray, my birthday too, lots of celebrations.
August, time to relax and enjoy the rest of the summer.
September, back to school, new one this year!
October, Hallowe'en and getting dark.
November, remember the war, getting darker.
December, Christmas yippee, pressies, sweets and Christmas pud.

Jennifer Harper (11)
Ashgrove Primary School

Ballet

Once I had a dream
That I was a famous ballet dancer,
Like Darcey Bussell
And danced in mid-air.

I wished I could dance with a partner,
That he could lift me up into the air
And throw me around and around
In the air.

I would dance my heart out,
Until I was tired, in my ballet dress
And my dance teacher would say,
'Lift her higher.'

I would love to dance
In the Grand Opera House
With lots of people watching me.
I would dance on my toes, on the very top,
Until my shoes wore out.

I hope this dream comes true some day
When I am older,
And all this that I have said.
So I am getting there, getting there, getting there!

Kathryn Fusco (10)
Ashgrove Primary School

RFC

Football crazy, football mad,
Go to Glasgow and see the Rangers' lads.
If they score, we will roar,
If they win we'll put the rest in the bin.
If they lose, we will boo,
Football crazy, football mad.

Debra Millar (10)
Ashgrove Primary School

My Brother, Samuel

My brother is called Samuel,
He is very, very stupid,
His brain is the size of a peanut
And he talks nonsense.

He is very, very weird
And so very, very crazy,
That sometimes I can't
Believe he's my brother.

He sometimes crawls around
On the floor playing doggy,
Or he jumps about
Like a monkey.

He likes playing with cars
And once he tried to get
Into one of the cars,
Which is very, very weird.

Samuel is my brother,
Which sometimes I can't believe,
But now I've learned to live with him,
But it's still a nightmare.

Thomas Baxter (10)
Ashgrove Primary School

The Mule Who Was Quite Cool

There once was a mule
Who was quite cool,
But didn't know how to dance.
So he went to the duck,
Who said that he sucked
And taught him to dance again.

Jade Anderson (9)
Ashgrove Primary School

Football

When I watch football on the TV,
They tackle, save and defend,
If I watch I could learn.

As they tackle, shoot and strike,
I hear the cheers and the boos,
They miss sometimes and score sometimes.

As they pass the defender
And try to strike,
They're going to score . . . oh no, they missed.

They slide and pass
And run with the ball,
They pass the defender

And . . . oh! What a goal!
People cheer and scream
And sing, 'Oh, what a goal!'

Jennifer McFall (10)
Ashgrove Primary School

My Poem Of The Months

January brings rain and snow
February brings love and caring
March is for giving and sharing
April brings us Easter bunnies
May is time for spring to appear
June is for shearing
July brings warmth and sunshine
August brings summer to an end
September leaves fall to the ground
October brings a lot of scary sounds
November is very dark and cold
December brings love, peace and joy.

Rebecca Gray (11)
Ashgrove Primary School

Fairy Poem

Beauty and the Beast
Had a big feast
They danced all night
And got a terrible fright
And then nodded off to sleep.

Cinderella is a maid
All her clothes have long since faded
Cleaning windows, dusting shelves
She's just like five slave elves
Always wishing in a well.

Pinocchio is made of wood
He is always in a good mood
Whenever his father is sad
Pinocchio will soon make him glad
With his friend Jiminy.

Sleeping Beauty went to sleep
Nobody ever made a peep
The rain and wind came and went
Then the friendly fairies sent
The prince came to save the kingdom.

Winnie the Pooh
And Tigger too
Walked about in the wood
And heard the owl twoot
And ran out looking terribly spooked.

Jane Hillis (10)
Ashgrove Primary School

Dolphins

Dolphins, dolphins, wild and free,
Dolphins, dolphins, come to me,
Dolphins, dolphins, in my mind,
Dolphins, dolphins, are very kind,
Dolphins, dolphins, love to swim,
Dolphins can sing and sing,
Dolphins are not one bit shy,
Dolphins love to smile and smile,
They love to play every day
And under the sea the dolphins are free
From all the fishing nets,
But sometimes they get caught and they,
Fight and they fight but they never quite get out,
So this is why I'm saying don't go playing
By the sea with your fishing nets.

Kerry Thompson (10)
Ashgrove Primary School

Football Crazy

I like to play football,
It is the best game,
I play it with all my best friends,
My favourite teams are Liverpool and Rangers.

The teams I hate are Celtic,
Because they are very wick,
I hate Glentoran, Donegal, Celtic,
They are wick too.

The people that scored the most goals,
Are Glenn, Jack and Callum,
They are the best people in our team
And Kyle, he is good as well.

Adam McAllister (10)
Ashgrove Primary School

Football Crazy

I like to play football,
My favourite player is David Beckham
And my favourite teams are
Liverpool, Manchester United,
Real Madrid and Rangers.
I really like Michael Owen.

All my friends love football too,
Especially Glenn, Matthew and Callum,
Adam and Kyle love it too.
We play football every day,
We all love it.

I really hate Celtic because
They are wick and I hate Glentoran,
Donegal Celtic, Cliftonville and Aberdeen,
I think they are all very wick.

Jack McWilliams (9)
Ashgrove Primary School

Harry Kewell

I like Harry Kewell
I think he's a good football player.
I like his celebration when he scores
I want to be like him.

He plays right midfield
He scored a header against Birmingham City.
He is my favourite player.

He is fast at heading the ball
He is fast at getting into position.
He is very cool looking when you see him
He is very kind.

Matthew Whittley (9)
Ashgrove Primary School

Where Should I Go Today?

Where should I go today?
I could go to the moon and play,
I could see the red planet
And have fun with the aliens,
No, maybe another day.

Where should I go today?
I could go to Egypt and play,
I could play in the pyramids
And swim in the Nile,
No, maybe another day.

Where should I go today?
I could go back home and play,
I could play with my friends,
Or even see my granny,
Yes, that's where I'll go today!

Melissa Boyd (9)
Ashgrove Primary School

Football Crazy

Football is the best in the land,
Every day it makes me glad.
Go and see them, fat and thin,
It's just enough to make them win.

Every day I play it somewhere,
We sometimes lose but I don't care.
We always win once a week
And my mum always writes the score on a sheet.

Football is the best,
Better than all the rest.

Lauren Lavery (9)
Ashgrove Primary School

Seasons

Seasons come at all different times
They are spring, summer, autumn and winter
The seasons are brilliant
And lovely every day.

Springtime is when the flowers come out
And little lambs are born
They come out to play
And dance every day.

Summer is very hot
And everyone goes on holiday
There could be a really bad heatwave
But that doesn't mean we can't play.

Autumn time is great
The leaves turn crisp and gold
You have to scrape them off your lawn
But it is great anyway.

Wintertime means Christmas time
The snow lies on the ground
Santa Claus comes down the chimney
Girls and boys love it
And the seasons end just there.

Elaine Uprichard (9)
Ashgrove Primary School

Travelling Poem

Travelling is fun
Travelling is good
The neighbourhood know it well
As shine is for good
Trains on rail
Planes in air
Flying so high
The kingdom of air.

Phillip Henderson (9)
Ashgrove Primary School

Horses

Horses are as cute as a teddy
And just as nice as a bowl full of jelly.
With fur as soft as a cotton wool ball,
You're my favourite out of them all.
They make me laugh and they're fun as well,
With a lovely long tail and mane as well.
I like them because they're gentle and soft,
But I wish I could keep them up in my loft.
Horses, horses, you're the best,
Better than all the rest.

Zara Morrow (10)
Ashgrove Primary School

Hallowe'en Is Coming On

Hallowe'en is coming on
And the pumpkins are so fat,
Would you please put a burger
In Scooby-Doo's hat!
The zombies are still dead
But the Grim Reaper's not
And in the ground he'll rot.
So enjoy the season
With a jolly good reason!

Ben Robinson (10)
Ashgrove Primary School

Winter Life

W inter is so white with the snow and the light.
 I n the winter all the time the snow is coming.
N ever ever is it bright when winter is in the night.
 T he leaves have fallen in a bell, you never will tell.
E very winter is never ever any better.
R obins ready themselves for winter weather.

Stefan Mullen (9)
Ashgrove Primary School

Pony Pal Peanuts

Pony pal Peanuts
Where have you been?
Pony pal Peanuts
Tell it to me.

I've been to Pony Club
The ponies are neat
They're jumping and having fun
We do the same thing.

I know, I know
You want to go
Let's get ready
For a show.

Thank you owner
Thank you owner
You know, you know
I love shows.

In the horse box you go
So we can go to the pony show
One hour, two hours, three hours, four
We've arrived, let's go, let's go!

Jump, jump, jump, jump
Faster! Go Peanuts, go!
Yes, we've won!

I love you
My pony pal Peanuts.

Anne Sheridan (10)
Ashgrove Primary School

Snow

It snows, snows, snows,
I love the way it glows.
Children throw snowballs
And then more snow falls.
My dog loves the snow,
You should see the way she goes.
Some people don't get to school,
It's very, very cool!
It glitters and shines,
Oh, so fine!
Snowflakes tumble
As the drumbeat rumbles.
Little robin redbreast
Rubs his cold little chest.
Snow is the best,
Better than the rest!

Christine Rea (10)
Ashgrove Primary School

Dogs

Some small, some tall,
Some bold, some gold,
Some black, some named Jack,
Some playful, some fierce,
Some brown, some chase their tails around,
Some puppies, jumping through puddles,
Some old, getting lots of cuddles,
Some great hounds, taking huge bounds,
That's what dogs are like.

Hannah Sullivan (10)
Ashgrove Primary School

Where Do I Come From?

Where do I come from?
I don't know.
Do I come from space
Or Porta Rico?

Where do I come from?
I doubt you'll tell me.
Do I come from a dog
Or a chimpanzee?

Where do I come from?
Tell me and be a good lad.
Do I come from a zoo
Or a top secret lab?

Where do I come from?
I don't want to think.
Because I could come from the toilet
Or the kitchen sink!

Bethany Doig (10)
Ashgrove Primary School

Best Friends

Best friends, best friends,
Who are they?

Best friends, best friends,
What do they say?

Best friends, best friends,
We all love to play.

Best friends, best friends,
They're the friends that are the best!

Rachael Lowry (9)
Ashgrove Primary School

Going To The Park

Going to the park
To have lots of fun
While my mum and dad
Will watch the sun.
Going on the steps
To go down the slide
Then going on the merry-go-round
Oh, what a ride.
Going on the climbing frame
To get to the top
Walking round the park
And sometimes doing the hop, hop, hop.
Going home I hear a dog bark
The place I want to go tomorrow
Is the park.

Garry Tilbury (9)
Ashgrove Primary School

Seasons

Spring, spring, let the bells ring,
Lambs are born and little girls sing.

Summer, summer, daffodils spring,
Little birds sing.

Autumn, autumn, my birthday is there,
Presents are on the table and a birthday cake as well.

Winter, winter, the last season of them all,
Everyone is playing in the snow.

Soon it will be spring again.

Lindsey Kerr (10)
Ashgrove Primary School

Spring Is The Best

S un in the sky
P raising the sky
R inging out the sunshine
I n and out of the clouds
N othing better
G etting sunny!

I n the yard
S un is great

T he sky is blue
H igh above the ground
E verything so beautiful!

B elieve it or not
E nough is enough
S pring is here
T he best season of the year!

Jordan Bustard (10)
Ashgrove Primary School

Leaving

Would you ever think
That someone might go
And leave you all alone
You're swarmed by people
But still feel alone
You never think about these things
Until they are near enough
For you to see
A snap of a finger
A sound of a machine
But you never think that someone might go
Leaving you all alone.

Fiona Brown (10)
Ashgrove Primary School

Look After Yourself

Eat plenty of vegetables
They're really good for you
Like carrots, sprouts and peas
And lots of others too.

Remember you should brush your teeth
To keep them nice and clean
Up and down and back and forth
A healthy teeth routine.

Find out what the weather is like
And if there is a chill
Make sure you wrap up warm -
You don't want to get ill.

Lastly jog around the room
Running's fun to do
Bob feels really healthy now
We hope that you are too.

Nicole Millar (9)
Ashgrove Primary School

World War II

Allies die and young soldiers cry,
The fight begins, Captain Higgins
Tells his men to go.
Nazis die and bullets fly,
Men blown up.
Planes fly as tanks roll by,
Jeeps beep and cities look like heaps,
Families very upset.
The war ends, turned round the bends,
Peace is finally restored.

Ian Hamill (10)
Ashgrove Primary School

Summer

Licking lollies,
Playing with dollies,
Kicking balls,
Climbing walls,
Always walking,
Non-stop talking,
Having continual fun
And bathing in the sun,
Riding bikes,
Flying kites,
Rowing boats,
Taming goats.

Watching divers,
Giving out fivers,
Being bad,
But never sad,
Eating food,
Being a cool dude,
Running races,
Making faces,
Paddling in the pool,
Breaking every rule,
Being a total fool
And utterly cool.
That's what summer's all about!

Lucianna Hughes (9)
Ashgrove Primary School

Little Miss Muppet

Little Miss Muppet
Sat on her bucket
Reading a scary book
Along came a monster
Who sat down beside her
And asked could he have a look.

Sian Allen (10)
Ashgrove Primary School

The Man From Japan

There was a man from Japan,
Who ran away in a can.
He had a plan,
A brilliant scam.
While at sea,
It occurs to me,
He lost his plan,
His brilliant scam.
This man from Japan,
Who ran away in a can.

Lindsay Meaklim (10)
Ashgrove Primary School

I Wonder

I wonder, I wonder
Why stars are in the sky.

I wonder, I wonder
Why babies can't fly.

I wonder, I wonder
Why I'm not in space.

I wonder, I wonder
Why my life is a maze.

Elizabeth Glenfield (9)
Ashgrove Primary School

Humpty Dumpty

Humpty Dumpty went to the moon
Humpty Dumpty sat on a spoon
When he came down
He went into town
Looking like a great big clown.

Jordan Quinn (8)
Ashgrove Primary School

Animals I Like

Foxes are bushy, furry and cute
Flamingoes are pink and they stand on one foot
Tigers are stripy with razor-sharp teeth
Orange on top and white underneath
Baboons have blue bottoms and they're ever so cheeky
Mice are so quiet except when they're squeaky
But the animal I like the best is
My dad in an old string vest.

Shannon Peoples (8)
Ashgrove Primary School

My Friends

My best friend is called Kerri
She's always very merry
But she does sit on a banana
With my other friend, Hannah
I'm good friends with Heather
Who's as light as a feather
Now come to me, I'm really funky
But I do admit I can be a monkey!

Julia Coulter (9)
Ashgrove Primary School

Rebecca

R abbits are my favourite animals.
E very day they eat fruit.
B ecky is my nickname.
E els are my second favourite animals.
C ats are very cute.
C oca-Cola is my favourite drink.
A pples are very healthy.

Rebecca Caldwell (8)
Ballygolan Primary School

The Legendary Dragon

The legendary dragon comes out only at night.
He fires away his dragon flames
When he sees the enemy.
He guards five crystal night lights,
He's fierce,
He's terrible,
He's a very angry dragon.
The world cannot defeat him,
Or stand up against his might.
Yes, the legendary dragon, he's so powerful.

Thomas McKee (8)
Ballygolan Primary School

Rachel's Poem

R abbits are my favourite animal.
A pples are very healthy for you.
C ornflakes are my favourite cereal.
H elicopters fly in the air.
E lephants are big with their trunks so long.
L ions are bad with their fierce roar.

Rachel Cochrane (8)
Ballygolan Primary School

The Wee Man

There was a wee man on the bus,
Who really was in a big fuss.
The fuss was so big,
That he gave me a dig
And I ended up losing my wig.
The driver said 'Run,
The man's got a gun,'
So I felt like a nun on the run.

Craig Graham (8)
Ballygolan Primary School

A Time Once Upon

Once upon a time,
I learnt a wee rhyme.
With a jelly bean,
That is very, very lean,
If you know what I mean.
But I am a treasure chest,
Full of information.
So come to me,
You will find the key,
To once upon a time,
I learnt a wee rhyme.

Samuel Waite (8)
Ballygolan Primary School

The Sun

The sun is bright
And shines its light,
Upon a great big world.
So close your eyes
And when they open wide,
You'll find an extraordinary sight.

Jamie Kirkpatrick (9)
Ballygolan Primary School

The Moon

There once was a man on the moon,
He really did look like a balloon.
His spaceship came up,
It looked like a cup
And out jumped his sweet little pup.

Andrew McGovern (8)
Ballygolan Primary School

Butterfly

Fly little butterfly fly so young
Your beautiful wings spread as you fly alone.
Butterfly, butterfly, spread your wings
The lovely colours as you fly, fly.
Oh lovely butterfly, fly away
Maybe you will come back some day.
Butterfly, butterfly, why are you sad?
I want you to come and we can be glad.
Forever and ever and where we will love
And treasure every little thing.

Rebecca Boland (9)
Ballygolan Primary School

The Alien

There was an alien at my door
With big fiery eyes
The size of pies

Where did he come from?
How did he get here?
Perhaps he's just here for the beer

He just stood there looking at me
So I invited him in for a cup of tea
What a pleasure that turned out to be

He ate an iced bun
And we had lots of fun
When the alien came to my door.

Michael Thompson (11)
Ballymoney Model Primary School

My Cousin, Jenny

Early in the morning
When Jenny wakes up,
The first thing she looks for
Is her little musical cup.

She claps her hands
When breakfast is done,
She is doing well for a little girl
Who has just turned one.

She is always happy
Except when you have to
Change her nappy.

When she watches TV
She won't see you or me,
Because she's too busy watching
'Winnie the Pooh, where are you?'

Tiffany Gage (10)
Ballymoney Model Primary School

Snow

Snow softly flutters down from the heavens,
Like white butterflies in the morning.
Silently falling on the rooftops,
Making no noise like my pet rabbit.
Covering footpaths and roads,
Putting icing on window sills and trees.
I put on my hat and coat,
I build a snowman.
When I come in, I'm very cold.

Jamie Forsythe (8)
Ballymoney Model Primary School

A Rhyme Through Time

The Viking ships were very tough
The Viking men were very rough

Tutankhamen king at nine
Lost the throne in twice that time

If there's one thing that we know
It's that the cavemen weren't half slow

Then the Aztecs were in order
Till the Spanish army crossed the border

The Romans tried to rule for years
Time after time it ended in tears

If I've learnt one thing about this rhyme
It's that life's been poetic all through time.

Steven McDonald (10)
Ballymoney Model Primary School

Hallowe'en

H appy children trick or treating
A haunted house filled with shrieking
L ovely sweets are being shared
L ively screams from people scared
O utraged folk
W atch children run
E njoying frightening everyone
E vening of fun and spooks
N ot a night for reading books.

Lucy Maxwell (11)
Ballymoney Model Primary School

Bowling

With the ball in my hand
I step up to the line
'Move over my friends
This game is mine.'

First I hold the ball steady
Then roll it with all my might
Can you believe it
I've got a strike!

It's my friend's turn now
'Oh no,' she mutters
'Please, oh please
Don't go in the gutter.'

She takes her two turns
She gets a spare
And I think to myself
I suppose it's only fair.

It's the end of the game now
It feels as if it's only just begun
She turns to me and says
'That was really good fun.'

Into the car now
It's still not that late
So it's off to the café
For some chips on a plate.

Gemma Linton (11)
Ballymoney Model Primary School

Rugby

Rugby is so cool,
Rugby is such fun,
All can enjoy rugby,
In rain or in the sun.

In rugby you can run with the ball,
Pass it from guy to guy,
You can kick it down the pitch,
Until you score a try.

Ulster play great rugby,
Ireland play it too,
Never support England,
Just shout *boohoo.*

If you enjoy rugby,
You watch it every day,
Don't feel bad about it,
Just get out there and play.

Mark Coulter (10)
Ballymoney Model Primary School

Bullying

A bully is a person
That doesn't really care,
Whether they hit or punch
Or perhaps just pull your hair.

A bully is a person
That doesn't really care,
Whether they hurt your feelings
Or just push you off a chair.

A bully is a person
Who doesn't like to be caught,
So tell your mum or teacher
Then the bullying will *stop!*

David Thompson (10)
Ballymoney Model Primary School

Summertime

Summertime is nice and hot
Children run about a lot
They like to play in the pool
Because it keeps them very cool

Water pistols fly about
People always scream and shout
Everyone is full of joy
So everybody says *yahoo*

Summertime is full of fun
All the children in the sun
Then at night it's time to end
And in the morning it starts again.

Brad McClenaghan (11)
Ballymoney Model Primary School

Puppies

I love all puppies
They are full of fun
If you've got a ball
They're ready to run.

They'll chase your feet
Or steal your sock
But they're well behaved
When they want their walk.

I love all puppies
Big and small
But none are like mine
My favourite of all.

Judith Kelly (10)
Ballymoney Model Primary School

The Trouble With Sisters

They talk too much
They have no brain
They shout a lot
And they're a pain.

When they're tired
They're a grumpy guts
And when they're not
They're absolutely nuts.

They always get the front
When we're in the car
Who do they
Think they are?

When we're watching TV
They fight over the chair
It's so annoying
But I don't care.

They boss me around
But they can't see
That's the part of them
That gets at me.

Siobhan Brown (10)
Ballymoney Model Primary School

A Ginger Cat

There was a young girl called Pat
Who had a big ginger cat
That lay on the path on a mat
Along came a truck
And Pat's cat was stuck
And now he is six feet covered in muck.

Jordan Connelly (11)
Ballymoney Model Primary School

The Storm

The storm had been going on all day,
It was as if the house was going to fly away!
I heard the thunder and saw the lightning,
Which made it much, much more frightening.
The rain was strong and hit the glass,
The wind was swaying the trees and grass.
I thought the storm was never ever going to stop!
It rained harder and smashed tiles on the rooftop.
I went to bed still shivering with fright,
My mum asked me if I would be alright.
I tossed and turned but finally got to sleep,
In the morning I woke up and heard a cheep.
Some birds were singing outside in a tree,
Then I realized the storm was over *yippee!*

Yasmin Walker (11)
Ballymoney Model Primary School

Alan Gordon

A is for *grade A* which would be good to score
L is for *loud* which my mum says I am
A is for *annoying* which I know I can be
N is for *nosy* which I always am.

G is for *girls* who I despise the most
O is for *optimistic* which I am not
R is for *rampaging* that I do on my PS2
D is for *dancing* that I do on my dance mat
O is for *odd* which I think my sister is
N is for *noodles* which I love for my tea.

Alan Gordon (10)
Ballymoney Model Primary School

Bad Weather

Wind blew at the trees,
A heavy gale, not a gentle breeze,
One fell down with a big loud crash,
As I looked out eating bangers and mash,
Then out the window to my delight,
The rain dried up and the sun shone bright,
But then I awoke from that beautiful dream,
I looked out the window and started to scream.

The rain came down heavy and fast,
I knew to look it was going to last,
I gave a sigh and said to my mum,
'It's going to be bad, I'll have no fun.'
Won't be going out to play
And the words I dreaded, 'No footie today'.

Andrew Hanna (10)
Ballymoney Model Primary School

To A Stranger Say *No!*

If you're at home alone
And someone knocks at the door
Don't answer it.
Let it go,
Unless it's someone you know.
If the stranger keeps knocking
Ring up a close friend.
Tell them about it
Don't even doubt it.
If they say, 'Ring up the police!'
You know you can play when the stranger's away.

Rachael Martin (10)
Ballymoney Model Primary School

Football Is My Chosen Sport

Football is my chosen sport
I play it every day.

Football is my chosen sport
Liverpool, the team I support
Finvoy the eleven I play for
Michael Owen the player I adore
I dream of the day that I can play
The Riise, Owen, Murphy way
Defender, midfielder, goal scorer too
On the field I don't mind what I do
Just to kick the ball and enjoy the game
Playing in my team is my aim
And if we've won when the whistle blows
Then there's not a happier team home goes
Dreaming of the day
That perhaps we'll be in the FA
That's my sport, what I hope to be
Footballer, football it's for me.

John Doherty (11)
Ballymoney Model Primary School

Sport

When it comes to sport I am the best!
Football, basketball and the rest.
When I have a ball,
I take it around people thin and tall.
At basketball I'll do the same,
Nobody can beat me at my game.
Challenge me and you will see,
That you cannot beat me!
How about that? I'll just say,
'I'm going to beat your team some day.'

Jonny Kinnaird (9)
Ballymoney Model Primary School

The Seasons

Spring, summer, autumn, winter
Are the seasons of the year
The summer season is the best
The sun shines bright and we run all night
Autumn's when the days get shorter
The leaves fall down and the weather frowns
Then comes winter with snow and ice
It does nothing but rain and that's a pain
But before we know it spring is here
The flowers are out and the children shout!

Aaron Lamont (10)
Ballymoney Model Primary School

A Girl's Best Friend

I have a dog called Honey,
Sometimes she is very funny.
She is getting slower because she is older,
But I love her just the same.
I take her out for walks
And when she sees a cat,
She forgets that she is old
And nearly pulls me off my feet.

Rebekah Knight (11)
Ballymoney Model Primary School

Mrs Robinson

Mrs Robinson is a blast
But she's far too fast
She's really, really smart
Especially at art.

Linzi Watton (9)
Ballymoney Model Primary School

Spring's Morning

When I woke up one morning
There to my surprise,
A little bird was sitting
With tears in its eyes.

When I looked out the window
There was sun instead of snow,
I whispered to the little bird
'Spread your wings and go.'

I looked across the golden meadow
The daffodils were bright and yellow,
I said to the little swallow
'Your mum you will have to follow.'

I put the swallow on my hand
Up she flew and did not land,
Now I can enjoy my day
As I know my little swallow is up and away.

Laura Witherow (10)
Ballymoney Model Primary School

It's OK To Tell

At 3pm that's when I see them again
I can't seem to get it off my brain
They're so big that I can't fight back
He threw a punch at me
And then I heard a crack
It was my friend standing up for me
He held them off as long as he could
And there a teacher stood
'Miss, will you please help me
They are going to get me'
Then the teacher walked away
And I kept saying anyway
Finally she got it sorted out
And they were taught a lesson without a doubt.

Andrew Mills (10)
Ballymoney Model Primary School

Mice

Mice are small and cute,
They are really, really minute.
Squeak, squeak, squeak, as they go around,
They love to hide and never be found.
They really, really hate cats,
My dad thinks they're like wingless bats.
They like to drink milk
And their fur is as soft as silk.

Shiona Rankin (10)
Ballymoney Model Primary School

The Bully

Because I'm fat and really small,
And he is really rather tall,
He calls me names like Titch and Stubby,
And other names like Wee and Chubby.
He kicked at me and took my money,
And all his friends thought it was funny.
But I finally decided to go and tell
And now he's the one with the bad luck spell.

Jade McElderry (11)
Ballymoney Model Primary School

Mo And The Crow

There was a young girl called Mo
Who had a dark black crow
Mo went upstairs
To play with her teddy bears
While the crow made up a show.

Nikki Boreland (9)
Ballymoney Model Primary School

Skateboarding

Skateboarding is my favourite thing,
A great deal of joy it does bring.
Crooked grinds, kickflips and plenty more,
Are some of the tricks in store.

To choose a deck is hard to do,
There's a choice of Alien Workshop, Habitat or Baker too.
The wheels come thick and thin
And bearings at all prices go within.

Don't forget you need trucks,
Will it be Grindkings, Ventures or Krux?
Screws and bolts have to be bought,
All to make a pro set-up.

Christopher Cunningham (11)
Ballymoney Model Primary School

Millie

My dog, Millie, is short and white,
She doesn't look fierce but she can surely bite.
She lies on my knee and watches TV
And looks as cute as cute can be.
She climbs on the sofa when Mum's not around,
When she sees other dogs she makes an awful sound.
My nanny gives Millie chocolate chip cookies,
She slips them to her when she thinks we're not looking.
For Christmas she got a new bed and rug,
When she goes to sleep she's as snug as a bug in a rug.
Millie thinks she's the boss of the house,
But when my baby cousin comes to visit, she's as quiet as a mouse.

Olivia Pethick (10)
Ballymoney Model Primary School

Speedy

My hamster is called Speedy
He is sometimes very greedy
He plays on his wheel
And eats a great deal

He runs in his ball
Down the length of our hall
He sleeps in the day
When I wish he could play

He climbs to the top
And falls with a flop
Give him a fright
And he is sure to bite.

Charlotte Ross (10)
Ballymoney Model Primary School

A Bad Game

Giggs hit a shot,
He really wanted a goal,
But sadly ended up hitting the pole.
He tried to score another,
But ended up in bother -
Their winger brought him down,
All Giggs could do was frown!
He tried to get up,
But he was too lame,
He sadly thought,
This is the end of my game and fame.

Mark Crooks (10)
Ballymoney Model Primary School

Car Mania

There's lots of different cars about,
BMW, Mercedes, Renault and Ford.
All have high speed and class,
You'll never get bored.

Diesel, petrol, electric or gas,
The choice is yours.
Different colours, red, white or blue,
Pick the one that's right for you.

Watch your speed on the busy roads,
The traffic police are stopping loads.
Keep your mph on the low side,
Or else you know you'll be hitching a ride.

From the Jag to the Mini,
They're different in size,
They all need an engine,
That would be wise.

Bumpers, exhausts, steering wheel and tyres,
Good grip on the road,
For a journey that's safe,
Buckle up, slow down and follow the Highway Code.

Darren Rennie (11)
Ballymoney Model Primary School

My Dog

My dog is white and fluffy
He is still a puppy
He has short ears and believe it or not
He's 21 in dog years
His name is Cracker
He is such a smacker
I love him to pieces
My mum says
'I wish we could get another'
It could even be Cracker's brother.

Meghan Christie (10)
Ballymoney Model Primary School

My Family

I have a dad called Alan
Who's only 21
But I know he's over forty
And just says that for fun.
My mum's called Shirley
And she is a real good cook
She also likes to cut my hair
In the latest trendy look.
I have a younger brother
Who loves to play football
And if you live in the Meadows
'Come and play with me,' he'll call.
And lastly, my brother Stephen
He's got a girlfriend now
But don't tell anybody
For there would only be a row.

Mark Lyons (10)
Ballymoney Model Primary School

The Circus

The vans and the lorries go passing by
The peak of the tent way up in the sky.

The lions and tigers sit on their stool
The man points his whip, you'd think it was school.

The elephant comes in plodding along
The parrot on a bike singing a song.

Everyone laughs at the sight of the clown
It's great to see the circus in town.

Kelli Morrison (10)
Ballymoney Model Primary School

Wacky Week

On Monday I go to hockey,
It always is such fun,
We group in teams to form a match
And around the pitch we run.

On Tuesday it's off to swimming,
Where I practise the front crawl,
There's time to splash and fool around,
That's what I like best of all.

On Wednesday I have netball,
Here's where we pass the ball,
But we must always remember,
Not to hit the wall.

On Thursday it's off to music,
Where we play instruments and sing,
Charlotte hits the tambourine
And I make the triangle ring.

On Friday I have dancing,
Irish dancing if you please,
I've done so much throughout the week,
I'm now falling on my knees.

Oh boy, I'm glad the weekend's here,
So I can have a rest,
I'll need to recharge my batteries again,
So on Monday I'll be at my best.

Emma Ferris (10)
Ballymoney Model Primary School

Bullying

B is for beating people up
U is for using bad language (sometimes)
L is for leaving people out
L is for letting others take the blame
Y is for yelling at people
I is for insults which hurt people's feelings
N is for nagging on about things that are not true
G is for gangs which most bullies come in.

Sarah Dempster (10)
Ballymoney Model Primary School

Wintertime

The winter season brings frost and snow,
But inside we're snug with fires aglow.
The red-breasted robin comes bobbing along,
Cheering us all with his festive song.

Squirrels hibernate till spring comes around,
Whilst hardly little snowdrops pop up through the ground.
Children are longingly wishing for snow,
With snowmen, sleigh rides and snowballs to throw.

Rachel McElfatrick (10)
Ballymoney Model Primary School

My Best Friend

V is for various problems she has helped me through
I is for such an intelligent person she is
C is for the coolest person I have ever met
T is for talking, which she does all the time
O is for our friendship, which will never end
R is for reading, she does that a lot
I is for her interesting life
A is for we will always be friends.

Jade Watton (9)
Ballymoney Model Primary School

We're Best Friends

There's Rachel and Meghan and Gemma, that's me
Our schoolmates call us 'the terrible three'
You'll often find us fooling around
At break time and lunchtime in the playground.

We're all very sporty and like to keep fit
On Wednesday at football we wear the school kit
On Tuesdays and Saturdays we go for a swim
So that at galas we can help our team win.

We like the same music and love to dress up
Especially on Saturday for the Beehive Youth Club
We've been really good friends since we were three
And I really do hope we always will be.

Gemma Glendinning (10)
Ballymoney Model Primary School

Family

F is for four, the number of sisters I have
A is for animals we have visited at the zoo
M is for the minutes I spend with my family
I is for ice cream, our favourite treat on our days out
L is for the love that we share with one another
Y is for every year that passes and how much closer we grow.

David Barkley (10)
Ballymoney Model Primary School

A Friend

A friend gives hope when life is low,
A friend is a place when there's nowhere to go,
A friend is honest,
A friend is true,
A friend is precious,
A friend is *you*.

Paige Walker (10)
Ballymoney Model Primary School

Summertime

I love summer quite a lot,
I love summer 'cause it's hot.
I love summer 'cause it's cool,
I love summer 'cause we get off school!

I love summer 'cause we can go to the sea,
I love summer 'cause we drink iced tea.
I love summer 'cause of the bright sunshine,
I wish it were summer all the time.

Terri Kelly (10)
Ballymoney Model Primary School

Family

F is for fun with my family
A is for all the wonderful holidays we go on
M is for more fun I have with my brother
I is for going to Portrush and going in the sea
L is for lovely presents that I get from my family at Christmas
Y is for having my family to take care of me.

Chantelle Caulfield (9)
Ballymoney Model Primary School

Family

F is for family and friends
A is for aunties and uncles
M is for Mum who takes care of me
I is for interesting which my family is
L is for laughter which they bring
Y is for young and old.

Victoria McGregor (9)
Ballymoney Model Primary School

Cup Final

Just one more chance
And we could win,
Then Liverpool will shoot
To the losers' bin.

The crowd all watch
Until we score,
Yes, that winning goal
Makes us scream and roar.

Dean Clayton (10)
Ballymoney Model Primary School

Going Mad

A rhyme takes time,
I'm really mad and
The teacher says don't be sad.

I see a pain inside my head.
'Oh no! It's rhyming time,' I said.

But just one thing I'm saying,
Rhyming time isn't paying.

Simon McKendry (9)
Ballymoney Model Primary School

The Pan Man

There once was a man,
Who lived in a pan,
Where everyone cooked their food.
He went out for a look,
Then stopped for a snoop,
(And fell in some soup,)
And that was the end of the pan man.

Laura McIlveen (9)
Ballymoney Model Primary School

Venus

Beautiful Venus, so bright and rare
Help me see aliens everywhere
All different colours
From blue to pink
Well Venus, tell me, what do you think?

Wonderful Venus, seen from afar
From here on Earth you look like a star
Bright as the sun
Small as a mouse
Please send your aliens straight to my house.

Magical Venus, brighten the night
Shine in the sky with your little light
Twinkle in the dark
But gone by the day
Would you let aliens come out to play?

Colourful Venus, what will you do
If we came over to visit you?
Would you be angry
Or filled with glee?
Would those aliens invite us to tea?

Beautiful Venus, so bright and rare
Help me see aliens everywhere
All different colours
From blue to pink
Well Venus, what do you think?

Gemma Fox (10)
Ballymoney Model Primary School

Matthew

M is for *Matthew*, my toddler brother
A is for *always* climbing things
T is for *Teletubbies*, his favourite show
T is for the *trouble* he always gets into
H is for his *happy* smile
E is for *entertaining* us all the time
W is for *wrestling* with me on the floor.

I wonder who he takes after?
Why, his big brother of course!

Thomas Knight (9)
Ballymoney Model Primary School

Bethany

B is for but why did *I* get split up
E is for she is enormous
T is for my brother, Timothy, who laughed when I told him
H is for her sister, Hannah (who is very annoying)
A is for artistic, which she always is
N is for not obeying rules
Y is for yowling, which she is good at.

Nicola McCollum (9)
Ballymoney Model Primary School

Ghost

G is for ghosts that haunt you
H is for haunted house
O is for open the door
S is for skeleton in the coffin
T is for Timmy zombie.

Dillon Connelly (9)
Ballymoney Model Primary School

Perfect

Perfect is like the clear blue ocean,
Perfect is like the world full of bubbles,
Perfect is like the blowing wind in your face,
Perfect is like the animals playing,
Perfect is like a newborn duckling spreading its wings,
Perfect is like a bright, sunny morning when I wake up,
Perfect are my friends, family and teachers,
Perfect is the Lord Almighty of the world,
Perfect is the entire world.

Albany Ferguson-Smith (9)
Ballymoney Model Primary School

Ferrari

F is for the fans
E is for the engine in the car
R is for the reigning champion
R is for the races
A is for all the cars
R is for raging up the track
I is for Italy, Ferrari's home.

Aaron McKendry (9)
Ballymoney Model Primary School

The Haunted House

There was a haunted house,
It sat upon the hill,
If you wanted to enter,
You entered at your will.
Young Johnny he did enter
And the story he did tell,
About the one-eyed witch,
Who sat upon her stool.

Ricki Stewart (9)
Ballymoney Model Primary School

Football

F is for football mad
O is for on the ball
O is for one ball
T is for tackle
B is for brilliant
A is for attitude
L is for Liverpool
L is for lively.

Jonathan Tweed (8)
Ballymoney Model Primary School

Hannah

H is for happy Hannah
A is for a big surprise
N is for the noisy table
N is for a nice friend
A is for apple juice she likes
H is for a happy birthday to you, Hannah.

Jenna-Leah Lynch (8)
Ballymoney Model Primary School

Toca MG

T is for the touring cars that race,
O is for overtaking drivers,
C is for the cars that spin round corners,
A is for the applause from the crowd

M is for the mighty motor engines
G is for the great MG!

Philip Linton (9)
Ballymoney Model Primary School

Teachers

Some teachers are big
Some teachers are small,
Others are cross
And some are very kind.

I'm glad I like my teacher
She really is quite kind,
And when she is cross
Well, I think I don't mind.

Some teachers do funny things
And teachers are boring,
Well, some of them are boring
Most of them are fun.

Well, I like my teacher
And that's really all that matters,
Out of all the teachers I have had
I think that she is almost the best.

Charis Wilson (9)
Ballymoney Model Primary School

Jenna-Leah

J is for jelly that my friend likes
E is for eggs that she likes
N is for knowing the answer
N is for the noisy table
A is for apple that she likes
L is for the line leader
E is for everything she does
A is for animals that she has
H is for hyper Jenna-Leah.

Hannah McKinney (8)
Ballymoney Model Primary School

Pearl Harbor

1941,
A date which shall live in infamy,
A day like any other one,
While Japanese planes made their entry.

Out of the clouds came red spots
And I mean quite a lot.
There were so many that even America,
Couldn't fight them off!

There were sudden cries for help,
As people were wounded and shot.
Even all the hospitals,
Had a second lot.

Over 3000 were killed,
In one single morning.
Robbed of their lives,
Without one single warning.

Johnny Allan (9)
Ballymoney Model Primary School

My Tropical Blue

In my tropical blue of wonder
There's hundreds of bubbles
And when it rains you hear no thunder
Because you have no troubles.

In my tropical blue of laughter
There're hundreds of beautiful whales.
You always see them after
My tropical boat sails.

In my tropical blue of life
There's always some kind of war.
Why does man live in strife?
We don't want any more.

Bethany Millican (9)
Ballymoney Model Primary School

My Family

In my family I have
A brother called Robert
A mum and dad called Mary and John
A pet called Ben, the dog
We like living in the countryside in Aghadowey
Across the road my granda and granny live
Across from them my aunt and uncle and cousins live
They live on a farm.

Lauren McIroy (8)
Ballymoney Model Primary School

Spider

Spider, spider, on the web
Weaving silk, making your bed
Up and down, round and round
Winding traps to catch your prey
Your prey lands gently on the web
You run out quickly, 'Get off my bed'
You bite your prey with venom
And it drops down dead!

Ryan Sweetman (9)
Ballymoney Model Primary School

Mother

M y mum is called Clare
O h! How stunning she looks with her short, dark brown hair
'T idy your bedroom,' she often says
H ow I detest doing this, especially on Saturdays
E very Sunday she makes me a freshly baked scone
R avenous as I am, I eat it until the very last crumb's gone.

Priyanka Kher (9)
Ballymoney Model Primary School

My Dog, Sparkle

My dog's name is Sparkle
She is so very cute,
I got her for my birthday
And play with her each day.

My dog's name is Sparkle
I love her very much,
She sleeps in a hat every night
And we never ever fight.

My dog's name is Sparkle
We always joke and play,
I don't make her eat dog food
And she travels in my hood.

Paige McClements (9)
Ballymoney Model Primary School

Lucky The Cat

Lucky is a cat
She is nice and furry
When she goes to sleep
She curls up in a ball.

She purrs and if you lift her
And she does not want you to
She will wiggle her tail
Or scratch you.

She is a white cat
And when she goes outside
She comes in with big black paws
And I have to clean them.

Danielle Gordon (8)
Ballymoney Model Primary School

A Dogfish Tale

A little spotty dogfish
Swims along one day,
Swimming fast and slow,
In Portballintrae Bay.

The little spotty dogfish
Tries to find food,
Eventually comes up with something,
Under a rotten piece of wood.

The little spotty dogfish
Swims to a hole in a rock,
He wonders, *what is the time?*
Of course he had no clock!

A little spotty dogfish
Swims along one day,
Swimming fast and slow,
In Portballintrae Bay.

The little spotty dogfish
Comes out again next day,
I watch him swimming along,
In Portballintrae Bay.

I came out again at 6.00
He wasn't swimming there,
Has he been eaten up
By a big, fat *bear?*

PS Of course not!

Scott Anderson (8)
Ballymoney Model Primary School

Amo

A is for Amo, the wee, amazing dog.
M is for mutt that never shuts up.
O is for obedient dog that does what he's told.

Danny White (9)
Ballymoney Model Primary School

I Love Horses

Horses, horses
They are everywhere
Galloping in the fields.
Horses, horses
Running, jumping and leaping
Over fences and hedges.
Horses, horses
So beautiful and strong
Yet so gentle and friendly.
Horses, horses
Their coat so silky smooth
I love them.

Danielle Stewart (9)
Ballymoney Model Primary School

Wind

A lion roaring
Feel cold
Wintertime
A wet day.

David Stirling (8)
Ballymoney Model Primary School

Wind

A werewolf howling,
The wind blowing,
I shut out the sound
And turn around
In my bed.

Jimmy Mariano (7)
Ballymoney Model Primary School

The Jungle

Tiger, tiger, eyes so bright
In the jungle of the night.

Monkey, monkey, swinging low
Through the trees so fast you go

Lion, lion, the jungle king
Head held high to be seen

Eagle, eagle, flying high
Above the trees up in the sky

The jungle is the home of many
Of animals all shapes and sizes
Birds, snakes and insects too
And many, many more surprises.

Peter Johnston (9)
Ballymoney Model Primary School

Bully

B is for *bold* bullies
U is for *unkind* actions
L is for shouting *loudly* at other people
L is for *lonely* bullies with no friends
Y is for *yelling* bad words.

Lucy McWilliams (9)
Ballymoney Model Primary School

My Pet Lamb

L is for my lovely lamb
I is for the interesting times we share
L is for her big, long, lanky ears
Y is for - I hope I can keep her for years.

Hannah Witherow (8)
Ballymoney Model Primary School

Star

Once there was a cat called Star,
Who loved to go out at night.
We didn't know what she was up to,
Until she got into a fight.

Her little paw was badly hurt,
Her tail was soggy wet,
She didn't even eat her food,
So we had to call the vet!

Dad was so worried,
That he came from the football match,
But Mum was standing screaming,
'Star, there's a mouse to catch!'

But now she's feeling better,
She's prowling round the house.
What's she trying to pounce on?
Oh catch that silly mouse!

Amber-Rose McIntyre (9)
Ballymoney Model Primary School

Butterfly

B is for your beautiful, big wings
U is for your unusual colours
T is for a tickly touch
T is for your tiny eyes
E is for everything you like to eat
R is for the roses that you land on
F is for the way you fly
L is for your lovely, symmetrical wings
Y is for you're so lovely.

Naomi Connelly (9)
Ballymoney Model Primary School

Cats Or Big Cats

I like cats
Any kind of cats
Big, little, wild
Any at all.

Cats miaow
That annoys
People
(Me too).

But big cats
Wild cats
They don't miaow
They *roar!*

I have a cat
Who does not
Roar
She is a little cat.

She had two kittens
One Phoebe, one Spike
One was furry
One was not.

I love cats
Any kind
Some people don't like them
But some people do.

I love all animals
Big or small
I don't like creepy-crawlies
I hate, hate, hate them all!

Lesley-Anne Hanna (9)
Ballymoney Model Primary School

The Wind

The wind roars like a dinosaur and sounds like a wolf howling.
It whistles through the trees and down chimney pots.
It ruffles hair and shakes the leaves off the trees.
When it blows cold, we feel it freeze.

At sea the wind sets the waves crashing.
All the boats head for safety in harbour.
The gulls soar up above in the skies,
Whilst the wind drowns out their cries.

Ross Jackson (8)
Ballymoney Model Primary School

The Wind

When it is a windy day,
The leaves fall off they blow away.
The wind it whispers through the trees,
We know that this is just a breeze.

When it is a wet and stormy day,
Your umbrella could blow the wrong way.
When the wind makes a howling sound,
We know that winter is around.

Sarah-Louise Leighton (8)
Ballymoney Model Primary School

Wind

The wind blows up your hair.
The wind is very noisy and not good.
The wind is very noisy and cold.
The wind is very bad because
The wind will give you a cold.

Emma Chen (7)
Ballymoney Model Primary School

Windy Days

Wind, wind, you are so noisy,
Wind, wind, you scare me stiff,
Wind, wind, cold wind,
Wind, wind, you make me so sad.

Wind, wind, good for washing,
Blows the clothes and makes them dry,
Wind, wind, tricky wind,
You blow my hat away.

Wind, wind, fast wind,
Paper blowing, leaves falling,
Wind, wind, naughty wind,
Leaves our garden in a mess.

Amy McMullan (8)
Ballymoney Model Primary School

The Wind

Wind, oh wind,
Where do you come from
And where do you go?
I would like to find out,
But I really don't know.
Where do you start
And where do you end?
Are you lonely and needing a friend?
Wind, oh wind, how can it be,
You're gentle, yet strong enough
To blow down a tree?

Peter Wilson (7)
Ballymoney Model Primary School

A Windy Day

On a windy day, I am annoyed with it
And sometimes not.
However, today it was different
Today it was so windy.
The doors were slamming
And the bins were wobbling and shaking.
The wind is like the sound of a lion roaring.
The leaves fall off the trees,
Even the trees bend over.

Daniel Christie (7)
Ballymoney Model Primary School

The Wind

The wind is very blowy
It can mess up your hair
When you're out in the wind
It can blow you everywhere.
Put on your hat and scarf
And keep your ears warm
Put on your winter coat
Before the windy storm.

Gillian Henry (8)
Ballymoney Model Primary School

The Wind

The wind blows and makes a noise
But I'm safe inside with my toys.
The wind will howl through the night,
While in my bed I'm wrapped up tight.
In the morning it's gone away,
I am happy now to get out to play.

Jolene McKinney (8)
Ballymoney Model Primary School

Wind

The wind is howling
Whoosh, whoosh!
The trees are blowing,
Leaves falling,
The wind is calling.

The noise of the wind
Is whistling in our ears,
Roaring, angry wind
Like a lion we hear.

Khara Rennie (8)
Ballymoney Model Primary School

The Wind

The wind is howling,
The trees are blowing,
The doors are creaking
And it is very cold.

We are all nice and warm,
In front of a big log fire,
Listening to the roar of the wind,
As the bins rattle down the street.

Jamie Hanna (8)
Ballymoney Model Primary School

The Werewolf

I was sleeping in my bed one night
When I was woken with a fright
It sounded like a werewolf howl
So I ran to the bathroom and hid under a towel
I said, 'my, there's a wolf in our shed,'
'It's the wind, silly, now go back to bed.'

Tristan Fox (8)
Ballymoney Model Primary School

One Windy Day

One windy morning I heard the wind roar.
I got up as soon as I heard it,
I went out to see what it was,
There was nothing there at all.

Nothing blowing,
Nothing rattling,
Nothing there at all.

At lunchtime I went outside to play,
The wind nearly blew me off my feet.
It knocked down my little brother,
I shouted, 'You silly old wind, go away,
So my brother and I can stay outside to play.'

Megan McWilliams (8)
Ballymoney Model Primary School

The Wind

When I lie in bed
And I hear the wind roar
I feel cold and angry
My head feels sore.

The doors will slam
The windows will close
Leaves fall off the trees
As the wind blows.

When the wind starts to calm
I feel happy and warm
I'm glad it's all over
That loud, scary storm.

Chloe Kelly (8)
Ballymoney Model Primary School

Ollie The Owl

Ollie the owl was happy
He was as happy as could be
He had a lovely home
In a great big tree

He had lots of fluffy feathers
To keep him warm at night
Feathers keep him gliding
When Ollie is in flight

Ollie was a good hunter
He loved to eat mice
I would rather eat chips
I don't think mice are nice.

David McGoldrick (8)
Ballymoney Model Primary School

The Owl

Sleeping quietly in your barn
Keeping away from harm
By day you sit and wait
Until it becomes quite late

At night a hunter you become
Rabbit, mouse, squirrel and vole
Hiding deep inside their holes
Searching with your brilliant sight
High up in the air on your flight

Soon morning comes
And you return to rest
Tomorrow another test
To keep your young safe and well
But who can tell?

Ryan Ennis (8)
Ballymoney Model Primary School

Owls In The Night

I am a barn owl
With a sharp beak,
I am a barn owl
With golden-white feathers,
I am a barn owl,
Who hunts all night long,
I am a barn owl
Who sleeps all day,
I am a barn owl
Who eats grasshoppers, mice and small birds
All night long.

Allister Anderson (8)
Ballymoney Model Primary School

The Owl

The fat, fluffy grey owl
Looks down from his tall tree,
Eyes as big as saucers.
He sleeps all day and is awake all night,
Keeping watch over his prey.
Tu-whit tu-whoo he calls,
Tu-whit, tu-whoo!

Hannah Graham (7)
Ballymoney Model Primary School

The Wind

When I hear the wind blow, it sounds like a howling wolf,
When I go outside to play, I feel tattered all the day,
Then it tumbles the bins like a grumbling feather,
It tosses the trees like a hair not brushed,
How peace is broken with the wind.

Parisa Robinson (8)
Ballymoney Model Primary School

Barn Owls

I was in bed sleeping,
I was woken by an *eeeek,*
A sound that an owl makes.
I looked out my bedroom window.
It was a barn owl.
It has golden-brown feathers
And a very sharp beak,
And great hearing,
Because it heard a mouse and twitched its ears.
Then it flew away into the forest,
To the tallest tree and went to sleep.

Timothy Woods (8)
Ballymoney Model Primary School

Owls

Owls fly at night
Through the wood
With excellent sight
And without a hoot.

Hunting their prey
Looking for mice
After sleeping all day
Mmm, that would be nice!

John Coulter (8)
Ballymoney Model Primary School

Owls

Owls are night birds
They are birds of prey
They have huge, round eyes
And a sharp beak and talons.

Thomas Pethick (8)
Ballymoney Model Primary School

Owls

Owls sleep in the day,
But at night they catch their prey.
Their face is shaped like a heart
And really they're very smart.
They live in a small hole in a tree,
Their big, round eyes always stare at me!
They use their sharp beaks,
To gulp up what they like to eat.

Roger Gage (8)
Ballymoney Model Primary School

The Wise Owl

The wise owl comes out to play,
The wise owl flies away.
In the barn it feels at home,
Where a mouse is set to roam.
On the beam he keeps an eye,
As he is about to fly.
A meal he knows is in the hay,
Mouse, you will never see another day.

Megann Crawford (7)
Ballymoney Model Primary School

Owls

Owls are very large birds,
With big, round, piercing eyes.
They sleep all day
And hunt all night,
Always alert for their prey.
With their long, sharp claws,
Nothing gets away.

Abbey Boreland (7)
Ballymoney Model Primary School

An Adventure In The Night

Last night an owl flew over our house,
He caught sight of a little white mouse.
He came down very fast,
Like a rocket about to blast.
The owl said, 'Let me have a bite,'
But the mouse said, 'No!' in fright.
The owl said, *'Eeeek!'*
The mouse said, *'Squeak!'*
The mouse ran into the night,
While the owl took off in a fright.
You could see the mouse in the moon's beam
And the owl's reflection in the stream.
I turned on the bright light
And saw the little white mouse.
The mouse ran into its hole,
While the owl flew off to look for a vole.

Cara McConville (7)
Ballymoney Model Primary School

Owls

Owls have pointy claws and beak,
Sometimes you can hear the babies squeak.
Owls live at the tops of trees,
Where you can see the fluttering leaves.
Owls eat a lot of mice,
A barn owl would think that's nice.
With eyes so big and bright,
They can see in the darkest night.
Owls' feathers are soft and brown,
Sometimes you see them on the ground.

Niamh Rankin (7)
Ballymoney Model Primary School

Owls

There are many different types of owl,
Who like to fly around at night and prowl.
They hunt for rats and voles,
In small and tiny holes.
The owl's eyes are large, they see well in the dark,
Their feet are strong and their claws sharp.
They have a strong, hooked beak,
Which helps them eat their meat.
They live in barns and hollow trees,
Hiding away so no one can see.
Some people call owls birds of prey,
I would like to see one someday.

Shannon Holmes (8)
Ballymoney Model Primary School

Owls

A barn owl lives in a tree
And sometimes in a barn.
It sleeps through the day
And comes out at night.
The owl has nice big eyes,
So it can see in the dark.

Jodie Wilson (7)
Ballymoney Model Primary School

Owls

Owls fly at night,
They have very good eyesight.
They eat little mice
And sometimes give you a fright,
Especially at night.

Alexs Hutchinson (7)
Ballymoney Model Primary School

Owl

I am an owl
King of the forest
Wisest of all animals
Flying above the trees
Rivers and fields
In the dark
I hunt my prey
Then I sleep
During the day.

Robert Smyth (8)
Ballymoney Model Primary School

Owls

Owls are big
And speckled brown,
They live in a barn
And hoot and howl.
And if you saw them in the night,
Their eyes would give you such a fright.

Kirbie McClenaghan (8)
Ballymoney Model Primary School

An Owl

A is for an admiral bird
N is for owls are nocturnal.

O is for observant as they watch their prey
W is for their wings that they spread so far
L is for lightly flying in the midnight sky.

Olivia McConaghie (8)
Ballymoney Model Primary School

Feelings

Happy is like the colour yellow,
When I see horses I feel very happy.

Angry is like the colour red,
When my brother winds me up, I feel like screaming at him.

Sad is like the colour grey,
A black mist surrounds me when I'm left out.

Love is like the colour pink,
When you're in love, it feels like you're floating on air.

Excited is like the colour orange,
It is bright and sparkling, like my uncle's wedding.

Guilty is like the colour black,
I feel guilty when my mum gets upset.

Victoria Price (11)
Brownlee Primary School

Feelings

Confusion like the colour red,
Answers and questions swimming around in my head.
Worries like the colour blue,
They make you feel like you are being pulled into the cold sea.
Excitement like the colour yellow,
A playful dog jumping up on you.
Helplessness like the colour black,
A thick mist building up all around you.
Anger like the colour red,
A devil messing around with my feelings.
Sadness like the colour grey,
Tears dripping from my eyes.

James Magee (9)
Brownlee Primary School

Friendship

F unny and caring
R eliable and trusting
I will always help them
E ver my friend
N ever talks about me
D oes things for me
S he will not lie to me
H ow she shares things with me
I won't lie to them or talk about them
P eople bully me but my friend sticks up for me.

Tara Townsley (10)
Brownlee Primary School

Friendship

F or giving me strength through thick and thin
R especting me even when I am nasty
I nterested in things I do
E very time I'm feeling down they pick me up
N ever-ending care
D ependable all the time
S haring and caring
H elpful and grateful
I nterested in what I say
P repared for me all the time.

Lauren Mason (11)
Brownlee Primary School

Friendship

F orgiving me when I'm nasty
R especting me
I ndependent but still cares
E very time I'm lonely she cheers me up
N ever annoys me
D oesn't always depend on me
S hares with me
H as faith in me
I nvites me to play with her
P rotects me.

Natalie Bresland (11)
Brownlee Primary School

The 11-Plus Test

It felt like a dragon taking over my body.
I felt like my heart would stop and never start again.
The 11-plus, I hated it the most.
So I am glad it's over.
But when I went in the room
I thought, *where is my good luck charm?*
Is it here or there? Panic!
The next test was hard.
When I got out I wanted to scream and shout,
'It's over!'
I hated the 11-plus.

Nicole Machray (10)
Brownlee Primary School

What Is White?

White is the mist on the mountainside,
White is the ice to slip and slide,
White is the cloud so vast and wide,
White is the dress of a beautiful bride.

White is a polar bear in the snowy land,
White is the warm and dusty sand,
White is the pebbles on a blowy strand,
White is the diamond in big demand.

White is paper ready for art,
White is a horse to pull a cart,
White is the cold to dull your heart,
White is a grape, sometimes tart.

Victoria Mayers (11)
Carr Primary School

What Is White?

White is snow, soft and crunchy under my feet,
White as the polar bear rolling in the snow,
White as the West Highland terriers as pets,
White as bulbs shining bright.

White as a lily growing in the field,
White as a piece of chalk writing,
White as a snowflake from flake,
White is the colour of ice in the wintertime.

White as a snow leopard ready to eat,
White as the paper to write on,
White as an opal, a stone in the ground,
White as Bonnie, ready to fetch.

Kristopher Wilson (10)
Carr Primary School

Our Home Meals

Our home meals,
Our home meals,
Lovely leeks,
Lovely leeks,
Brilliant beans,
Brilliant beans,
I love it,
Another helping quick.

Robert McGibbon (8)
Carr Primary School

Jasper

I have a cat called Jasper,
He's orange, white and cream.
He lets me sit and stroke him,
While I just sit and dream.
I love my little feline friend,
He's older than I thought.
He was just a tiny kitten,
The day that he was bought.

Matthew Stewart (10)
Carr Primary School

Yummy

Yummy melon,
Yummy melon,
Yummy plums,
Yummy plums,
Yummy bananas,
I feel great!

Claire Windrum (7)
Carr Primary School

Tea

Tea, glorious tea
With sugar or milk
Tea, glorious tea
Tea is not for me
I prefer coke but
It makes some people
Boke
Tea, glorious tea
Tea
Is
Not
For
Me!

Matthew Stewart (10)
Carr Primary School

Food We Eat

Food we eat,
Mushy mush potato,
Green peas, I see out at sea,
I like my food, it's great,
I love it, *yum, yum!*
I eat my food,
Without any trouble,
Because it is loveable.

Heather Earney (9)
Carr Primary School

Food, Glorious Food

Food, glorious food,
All different shapes and sizes,
Food, glorious food,
All different tastes and surprises,
Some taste yuck,
Some taste delicious,
But all we need is food, food, food.

Andrew Mills (8)
Carr Primary School

Spiders

Spiders, spiders everywhere
Spiders in your bed
And under the stair
Spiders, spiders everywhere.

Spiders, spiders everywhere
Spiders in your hair
And down your underwear
Spiders, spiders everywhere.

Jonathan English (10)
Carryduff Primary School

Spiders

Spiders are very creepy
When people see them they turn weepy
Spiders are black
When people see them they give them a whack.

I see spiders go down the drain
Then the next minute, they come back up again.

Lee Waring (11)
Carryduff Primary School

Song Of The Christmas Tree

Christmas tree, Christmas tree sitting in my room with me.
Christmas tree, Christmas tree sitting with you and me.
I like to buy my Christmas tree.
I like to put it in my room with me.

Christmas tree, Christmas tree sitting in my room with me.
Christmas tree, Christmas tree sitting with you and me.
It is fun to put the lights on.
I love them when they flash.

Christmas tree, Christmas tree sitting in my room with me.
Christmas tree, Christmas tree sitting with you and me.
I love opening my presents by my beautiful tree.
I love Christmas because it has Christmas trees.
Christmas tree, Christmas tree sitting in my room with me.
Christmas tree, Christmas tree sitting with you and me.

Lee Graham (11)
Carryduff Primary School

The Ghost

The ghost is creeping down the hall,
With clanking chains and scary call!
Its only goal is to scare you, destroy your pride, your ego too!
Its origin is quite unknown,
Its locked the doors, made dead the phone,
You're trapped in the house with this creepy spectre,
That cannot be hunted with any detector,
The answer my friend, is to simply ignore it,
The lack of attention should very soon bore it,
It will leave your house to no one's dismay,
Where it cannot scare, it cannot stay!

Richard Bradfield (11)
Carryduff Primary School

I Found A Mouse In My Room

I found a mouse in my room and it is not the only one,
For I found a couple chewing away at, my big baked bun.
They ate it all up and then ate some more,
As I found some more nibbling on the floor.

I hate mice they're so small,
Unlike me I'm very tall.
I hate the way they creep and crawl,
Even if I put them in a ball.

I hear them nibbling beneath my feet,
It makes me shiver when I see them eat.
I hate mice they're so bad,
When the trap catches them I'm so glad.

So there is only one more thing to say:

I hate mice every single day!

Anna Marshall (11)
Carryduff Primary School

Poem Time

When it comes to poem time,
Or anything to do with rhyme,
My mind goes absolutely wild,
With sights and smells, strong and mild,
'Cause poems can be anything,
A dragon or a diamond ring.
Acrostic or a limerick,
Or a character called Rick,
A bird with golden feathers
And all sorts of weathers
And they are so fun to write,
In the day or in the night!

Sarah Gowen (10)
Carryduff Primary School

Flies!

Flies, flies everywhere in the garden and in the air,
Lots of people hate them so no one knows where they go
In the garden, in the park, down the lane, in the dark
We don't like them when they are near
I just wish they'd
Disappear!

Flies, flies all different kinds, they all have little, tiny minds
They must be hungry every day, oh please can you just go away!
They always fly around our food not knowing where they should
They are always flying around my head
I'd just wish they'd
Go to bed!

Flies, flies all different colours some of them might be brothers,
We hate them and they hate us so
What is the
Big fuss?

Abigail Magowan (11) & Charlotte McCune (11)
Carryduff Primary School

Pets

Some have fur, some have skin
Some like to look in the bin
Some purr, some bark
Dogs get walked in the park.

Some like to play
Cats like to go astray
Some like the wet
It's great to have a pet.

Throw a ball, see them run
They like to have a lot of fun
They like to eat food
Some think it's really good.

Mark Carson (10)
Carryduff Primary School

My Light

I have a light
It shines as bright as can be
And my little light
It helps me to see.

And when I'm lost in sin
And no one's there to help me out
My little light will be there
And that's without a doubt.

And when I'm all alone
And no wants to be my friend
My little light is going to help me
And that's to the very end.

And who's my little light
I can hear you say
Why, it's the Lord Jesus
My light, day by day.

Lauren Hall (11)
Carryduff Primary School

Bugs Bunny

Bugs is tall and skinny too
Walking around with a
Carrot in his mouth.

With long, floppy ears
He looks like a cloud
With his favourite words of
'What's up Doc?'

While eating carrots
There's a gunshot
He runs down his hole
To hide.

Jamie Patterson (11)
Carryduff Primary School

Animals

Animals are big
Animals are small
Animals are everywhere
Even at the mall.

Animals are fat
Animals are slim
Animals are everywhere
Even in the gym.

Animals are pleasant
Animals are smelly
Animals are everywhere
Even in my jelly.

I like animals
Maybe you do too
I like animals
Especially at the zoo.

Emma Payne (11)
Carryduff Primary School

Bees

Bees, bees buzzing bees,
Buzzing all around,
Stinging lots of people,
Making kids cry.

Bees are yellow and black
And have a tail which has a sting.

Bees, bees are buzzing
Bees that are sure to sting you!

Darren Lawthers (11)
Carryduff Primary School

Tiger

I have a kitten his name is Tiger,
When I stroke him he always likes to purr.

He likes to play with his ball
And curl up in my nanny's shawl.

He sometimes scratches me but not that much,
He has a kind and gentle touch.

When he eats he gobbles it down,
He has now time to make a frown.

When he finishes he goes out to play,
He'll come in later that day.

So later on he comes in to sleep,
He doesn't make one little peep.

So tomorrow this will happen again,
He will always be exactly the same.

Zoe Harron (11)
Carryduff Primary School

Family Photos

When I look at family photos
I'm looking back in time.
When I was small and not at all tall,
I rearrange my mind.
My brother, six, and me, just one,
I'm glad I'm not the only one.
But when I look at family photos,
All I see is . . . *me!*

Susan Hunter (10)
Harmony Hill Primary School

The Bug

There once was a bug,
Who had a rug
And was ever so snug in that rug.

In the springtime,
That bug had a dime
And bought a gold mine.

In the summertime,
That bug grew a lime,
In a very, very short time.

In the autumn time,
That bug turned nine
And ate his big lime.

In the wintertime,
That bug had a rhyme
And it sounded just like mine.

Rachel McCulla (10)
Harmony Hill Primary School

Moonlight Song

Suddenly I heard
The most beautiful birds
Swift and soundly through the night
This was the song of the dancing moonlight
The light of the stars twinkle in the sky
While the love sinks between you and I
The river is whispering
Your eyes are glistening
How I hear
When the song grows deeper far and near
How this night is so bright and clear
And why I need to tell you
I love you, my dear.

Michelle Roberts (10)
Harmony Hill Primary School

Why Bother?

Why bother to pick up litter
That's lying on the ground?
To put litter in the bin, what's the point?
Why don't you just leave it around?

Why bother to use unleaded,
When there's diesel and leaded instead?
It costs even more, but
As long as I fill this old shed.

Why bother to wash things at 40 degrees?
Even 60 to 80 will do.
It costs more money to use energy
And harms the environment too.

Why bother to put on a jumper,
When instead you could turn up the heat?
It costs even more and it's not just a chore,
Put on an extra pair of socks at least.

Why bother to do that recycling,
That paper, the bottles and cans?
Just throw them away and go out and play
And try not to dirty your hands.

So why do we have to recycle,
Re-use and reduce all our waste?
It's so we can save the environment
And make this a much better place!

Ben Johnson (10)
Harmony Hill Primary School

Snow Acrostic

S ee the white snow
N ever without its glow
O h! how lovely it looks,
W e'll stop reading our books.

Joshua Porter (8)
Harmony Hill Primary School

Dreams

Day breaks through,
Nightfall has gone.
The sun's rays shine through my window
And awake me from my dream.

The dream of me flying high,
Soaring over the treetops like a bird.
Or the dream when I'm a princess
And all the maids are doing everything for me.

But no, this wasn't my dream.
My dream was this:
I'm dirty and dressed in rags,
I pinch myself to wake up but I don't,
It wasn't a dream,
It was a day's work at the mill.

Paula McCalmont (10)
Harmony Hill Primary School

Winter Feelings

In winter I feel very weary,
It often makes me feel dark and dreary.

Wet and wind,
Snow and sleet.

There's never any sunshine,
To brighten up my street.

Cloudy skies, no children out playing,
Always wishing this weather wasn't for staying.

Oh well, let's not get too upset and sad,
Because spring will be here soon
And I'll be very glad and not too sad.

Shannon Rea (10)
Harmony Hill Primary School

A Hole In The Ozone Layer!

Our planet is dying!
And we all know why,
There is a great big hole
In the ozone layer, in the sky!

Our scientists can cure us of many diseases,
Our government spends millions on wars and defences.
But they should be sorting the ozone layer *now!*
It will be too late when they start and our planet will *die!*

They are the people who know how to fix the hole,
They are the people that can save our homes!
They have the technology they know what to do,
We can do things to help stop it, like re-using and recycling too!

But when it's too late to save our planet,
We know what the world will decide!
They will all have a meeting and panic and worry,
About the hole in the *sky!*

Stewart Gavin (10)
Harmony Hill Primary School

My Dream Car

I have a dream to own a car,
I would like it to be a TVR,
With buttons and gadgets in all the right places,
The red paint gleaming to show all their faces,
The seats will be black, soft, smooth leather,
The bumpers all shiny, glittering in the sunlight,
My foot will hit the pedal and off I'll race,
The round, fat, black tyres screaming as they pick up the pace.

Christopher Moore (10)
Harmony Hill Primary School

A Night On The Tiles

In the morning when your cat's crying on the doorstep
And begging to come in,
Have you ever wondered why he's got that glazed look in his eye,
As he passes you by on his way to the nearest warm bed?

Well, here's the reason:

That miaow of indignation you get at night is all just an act,
He really wants out!

That thump you hear when you're lying in your bed isn't the rain,
But your cat instead,
When all cats have gathered from neighbouring parts,
The party begins,
Paws start tapping and tails entwine,
All cats are having a wonderful time,
Dancing and singing the night away to their latest chart hits.
As dawn breaks, dark shadows can be seen slinking
And staggering to neighbouring parts.

So when he returns from his night on the tiles,
All bleary eyed with a glint in his eye,
You will know why!

Emily Smith (10)
Harmony Hill Primary School

Quarrelsome Kittens

Standing by the window in a big, big house,
Two tiny little kittens fighting over an innocent mouse,
The screeching of the two, the fierce little things biting
And scrabbling and even nabbing the poor mouse all chewed apart,
The two tiny little creatures looking over at it with despair,
Sulking with boredness and loneliness too,
They'll never learn, that's why they are two tiny,
Cute, funny, playful, little quarrelsome kittens
And that's just that!

Carrie-Ann Brady (10)
Harmony Hill Primary School

Sasha

Small and black,
Long, curly hair,
Two shaggy ears,
Tiny, cold, wet nose,
Two dark eyes,
Four soft paws,
One winding tail,
Loveable and huggable,
That's my pet dog,
Sasha!

Nathan Adams (9)
Harmony Hill Primary School

Bird Catcher

Large blue eyes
Steady body
Ears up high
Ready to pounce
Proudly!
Poor little bird!

Rebekah Leathem (9)
Harmony Hill Primary School

Snow Acrostic

S oft snow has fallen
N ow the ground is all white
O ld grandpa's stay inside
W hile others play outside.

Rachel McGrath (8)
Harmony Hill Primary School

Quick Cat

My cat is a sneaky cat.
Around all night
Looking for field
Mice. He jumps.
He leaps quickly
And creeps slowly
To strike for his food.

Christopher Ferguson (9)
Harmony Hill Primary School

A Shy, Little Cat

Ginger and thin.
Frightened.
Pointed ears
And big blue eyes.
A little shy cat.

Nicole Brown (8)
Harmony Hill Primary School

Fat Cat

Small, fat cat
Crawls swiftly
Leaps quickly
Pounces fiercely
Poor, innocent bird.

Ross Walker (9)
Harmony Hill Primary School

Moving

Boxes, boxes everywhere,
Upside down and everywhere,
Wish we weren't moving,
To our new house with our mouse.

Boxes, boxes everywhere,
Upside down and everywhere,
Mum, where's my bike?
I want my kite.

Boxes, boxes everywhere,
Upside down and everywhere,
I see boxes in my sleep,
I see boxes down my street.

Boxes, boxes everywhere,
Upside down and everywhere,
Our new house with our mouse,
Oh no! Boxes, boxes everywhere.

Marcus Sedman (9)
Harmony Hill Primary School

Fireworks

Shooting up into the air,
Sizzling, banging and dangerous, beware!
Catherine wheels and rocket ships
To set them off, just light the tips.

Standing in the cold and dark
Listen, *whoosh! Bang! Spark!*
We watch them light up the sky
They turn and whirl when they fly.

Bang, bang, bang, bang
The big finale - wow!
They fizzle out and leave
A still and cloudy sky.

Anna Jones (10)
Harmony Hill Primary School

The Worst Thing I Have Ever Seen

All day, all night,
My brother is acting weird.
He stares and stares,
I wonder what's going on?
Then, last Friday,
He came home with a girl,
Holding her by the hand.
Then he took her to the sitting room.
I crept after him, curious what was going on,
I had a look, the television was on.
They sat on the sofa,
My brother put his arm around the girl!
They stared at each other for a millisecond.
They got closer and closer!
It was horrible!
Then they . . . they kissed!
I nearly threw up!
I'll treasure that forever!

Siân Porter (9)
Harmony Hill Primary School

The Short, Sleek Cat

The short, sleek cat
Wanted a big rat
It leaped lazily
Over the wall
He got the rat
And the family
Was smiling proudly
At the cat.

Andrew McStea (9)
Harmony Hill Primary School

Life Through A Baby's Eye!

As I lie here in my crib
    A giant picks me up and puts on my bib
I now know it's time for tea
    As they are all surrounding me
I pick up the sticky stuff in front of me
    Then I throw it and laugh with such glee
I hear a splat and then a groan
    I get put in the playpen and start to moan
Teddy's here and his big bow tie
    Dolly breaks and I start to cry
I start to moan and groan and cry
    That's the life through a baby's eye!

Alicia Whitworth (9)
Harmony Hill Primary School

Unicorn

Fly away on mountain high
Eyes the colour of blueberry pie.
With winds of all colours
It stuns many others.
She comes down to land
On lovely golden sand.
Walks along with lots of others
One her mother and one her brother.
Up they fly into the sky past the moon
Look at them zoom, be home soon.
We watch as they disappear into the clouds
A thundering of feet so very loud.

Natalie Nicol (10)
Harmony Hill Primary School

When The Lights Are Out!

I say goodnight to my mum,
I kiss my dad on the cheek,
My mum turns the light off,
I hide underneath my sheet,
You see you are not the same as I
For when the lights are out
I want to cry
The dark is my very first fear
But most of all when no grown ups are near
I lie there in the dark,
No light,
Nope, not a spark,
Then I slowly fall asleep
I didn't cry!
I didn't weep!
The morning comes at last!
Wow!
Wasn't that fast!
Even though I'm only small,
I don't think it's too bad at all.

Rachel Devenney (10)
Harmony Hill Primary School

Winter

The sparkling snowflakes drop from the open sky
As the sun disappears into the ebony night.
Immense, glittering stars twinkle in the night sky
While children sleep with excitement
While their stockings swing from side to side above the open fires.
Grass is getting buried every second by the soft, white snow.
Sharp icicles are dripping in their dark, dull caves
Waiting for that moment when the sun comes through
And they'll melt into translucent puddles on the freezing floor.
Echoes haunt the Tundra Mountains as wolves howl
At the glimmering moon.

Sam Coates (9)
Harmony Hill Primary School

Seasons

Summer

Summer is a time of joy
When there is no school,
When the sun shines all day.
You can play with your friends
And forget about everything else!

Autumn

Autumn is a time of fun,
When you play in leaf piles
In the evening sun.
When you have picnics in the park
And you can play in the garden until dark.

Winter

Winter is a time of coldness.
When you wake up, the world is white.
When you walk you slip on the ice.
You have snowball fights with friends
And build snowmen in the garden.

Spring

Spring is a time of newness
When baby lambs are born.
When the flowers sprout their buds
And the trees blossom with leaves.

Olivia Wilson (10)
Harmony Hill Primary School

Mighty Cat

Small, thin cat
Scrambles suddenly
Leaps proudly
Creeps slowly
Poor little bird.

Sophia Reynor (8)
Harmony Hill Primary School

The Cat That Did Terrible Things!

Small, yellow eyes.
Small, ginger, fat body.
Slowly walking around the field.
Then pounces and leaps upon . . .
The small, baby bird
And walks around proudly
With the poor baby bird in his mouth.

Megan Herdman (9)
Harmony Hill Primary School

The Evil Cat

Big, fat cat
With big, red, evil eyes.
Crouching down
Getting ready
To pounce
On an unsuspecting
Mouse.

Jessica McKnight (8)
Harmony Hill Primary School

Cat

Big, green eyes
And a big, fat body
With ears sticking up
With legs crouching
And a poor, little
Bird.

Amy Hamilton (9)
Harmony Hill Primary School

Jewels

Tall, thin cat.
Which has lovely blue eyes.
White with big spots with a sleek coat.
Ears pricked up.
Creeps up on a poor, unsuspecting blackbird.
Walks away proudly, with the bird in his mouth.

Nicola Annett (9)
Harmony Hill Primary School

Slender, Young Tortoiseshell

Small, tortoiseshell cat.
Stealthily creeps across the lawn.
Quickly pounces
And grabs the ignorant bird.
Trots home proudly.
With the bird hanging limp in its jaws.

Stuart Wilson (9)
Harmony Hill Primary School

Oscar The Cat

Fat, lazy cat.
Loves his food.
Mmm delicious!
Now time for a nap.
But one problem . . .
I am too fat for my cat basket!

Danielle Agnew (9)
Harmony Hill Primary School

The Cat

Small, little body.
Small, blue eyes.
Pricked up ears.
Crouches down low.
Hunts suddenly.
Poor, little bird.

James Dowse (8)
Harmony Hill Primary School

My Cat

Tall, black and orange cat
Having a nap.
Curled in a ball.
Snug as a bug
In a rug.

Ashleigh Patterson (9)
Harmony Hill Primary School

Limerick

There was once an old man
Who sat on a can
He went to space
And lost his waist
And that was the end of the man.

Thomas Smyth (9)
Linn Primary School

Happiness Is . . .

Happiness is at the end of the day,
Lying in a bath
When I can forget all about
My English and math.

Happiness is on a cold winter's morn,
Feeling the warmth of my bed
And the look of a rainbow,
Colours of blue, green and red.

Happiness is when the sunshine appears
And kisses all the flowers,
When April comes along
And brings with it some showers.

Happiness is being with my friends,
Talking about showbiz,
Put all these things together
And that's what happiness is.

Hayleigh Brereton (11)
Linn Primary School

Who Is It?

Who is it that
Puts glue on my bed
Breaks my cupboard
And takes my ted?

Who is it that
Steals my money
Takes my clothes
And calls me honey?

Who is it that
Feeds my rabbit
Closes the gate
And stops my habit?

Louise Wylie (11)
Linn Primary School

Exams

'Begin!' says the teacher,
As silence falls.
The clock ticks slowly,
'You have an hour!' the teacher calls.

Everyone's nervous,
I can hear my heart beat.
Kerry throws a note,
Jennie fidgets in her seat.

Time is running out,
I try to think.
John drops his pen cartridge,
My paper is covered in ink.

One more question,
'Stop!' the teacher screams.
I put down my pen,
I'll get an A in my dreams.

Alice Cameron (11)
Linn Primary School

No Way!

No way am I going to
Wash and clean the floor
To tidy up my things
Or varnish the door.

No way am I going to
Iron my shirt
Clean up my desk
The house is full of dirt.

No way am I listening
I'm not doing that
So my mum came over
And hit me with a bat.

Aimée Agnew (11)
Linn Primary School

The Seasons

In spring, little lambs are born,
When baby birds sing their lullaby song.
When buds on trees pop out to say,
'Hello, how are you, on this fine spring day?'

In summer we are off school
And little children play by the pool.
It's when we eat lollies or ice cream
And sit and sunbathe or even daydream.

In autumn the leaves are falling,
Which makes us go a yearning,
To collect conkers from the ground
And show off what we have found.

Winter is that time of year
For happiness, love and lots of cheer.
With the rain and sometimes snow
Everybody will know -
Winter is my favourite season,
I like the snow, that is my reason.

Tracey Todd (11)
Linn Primary School

The Wolf

As the wolf howls at midnight,
All the creatures run at the terrible sight,
The wolf as ferocious as can be,
The creatures run, scatter, they flee.
The wolf prowls off the rock and into the forest,
In fear the birds small and large chorused.

It runs as it sniffs the forest floor,
It feels as if it's heart has been tore,
For people think it's such a cruel creature,
It sinks into blackness, lower and lower, deeper and deeper.
But the wolf is actually very bright, it's noble too,
But the final decision is up to you.

Ryan Campbell (10)
Linn Primary School

My Dog, Ted

My dog, Ted has a brick for a head,
He wears it on walks, he wears it in bed.
Even though he's the cutest thing,
When it's autumn he thinks it's spring.

'Fetch the ball!' I would say,
But Ted my dog, looks the other way.
When he sits on Mum's lap all day long,
If I cry he things nothing's wrong.

When I take him on long walks,
Ted, my dog, always stops.
If there is another dog in sight,
Ted thinks it's playing when it bites.

On Saturday morning when I'm not at school,
Ted snuggles in my blankets of wool.
Ted is not what you'd call so bright,
But I think the decision I made getting him, was right.

Victoria McFetridge (11)
Linn Primary School

My Big Brother

My big brother is a pest
My life is like one long test.

My best friend's brother is so cool
Compared to mine who is a fool.

He's like a car that just won't start
I wish he'd just fall apart.

He thinks he's tough like a piece of rubber
He pushes me around like I'm old blubber.

When I put something in the bin
He comes along and pushes me in.

Zoe Zolene Mayberry (10)
Linn Primary School

Who Is It?

Who is it that
Eats my sweets,
Yells in my ear,
Pinches the meat,
When no one is near?

Who is it that
Messes up my room,
Breaks my toys,
Makes me feel gloom,
Is it all those awful boys?

Who is it that
Breaks into my safe,
Steals my money
And spills honey,
All over the place?

Who is it that
Scribbles on my books,
Uses my best top to wax their bike,
Is always saying I can't cook -
Could it be all down to Mike?

Patricia Leitch (11)
Linn Primary School

Granny Ginger

Granny Ginger has bright orange hair,
1990s green glasses but she doesn't care.
She has a husband called Mr Ginger
And a daughter called Ruth,
She also has a shiny gold tooth.
She drives an ancient mini with no radio at all,
Which also couldn't get her as far as the fruit stall.
My opinion is that she's a balloon,
But you have a good think
And I'll see ya soon.

Scott McClelland (9)
Linn Primary School

Who Is It?

I hear the door open,
In comes the breeze,
I am alone in the house,
Except for my mum, Denise.

My mum's in the kitchen
Baking some bread,
'Anybody in?'
Is what it said.

I open my door
And creep down the stairs
I reach the bottom
The figure glares.

I run back upstairs
To get my breath back
This person is coming
With a tiny sack.

I jump on top
The figure screams
The figure shouts, *'Stop!'*
Mum shouts up, 'Anyone for custard creams?'

Mum comes up and says to me,
'How evil can you be?
I forgot to tell you
I invited Gran for tea!'

Hannah McKay (10)
Linn Primary School

Winter

Winter is the time of year when snowflakes fall from the sky.
Cold and icy the ground will be when it snows all around.
Children playing in the snow having so much fun.
Mum calls time for tea, but we just play on.

Grace Clements (10)
Linn Primary School

Getting A Pet

My mum says
I can get a pet
But I don't know
What to get.

My mum wants a
Cute dog or cat
But they're too normal
I want a bat!

But my mum
Does not agree
Although she said
It was up to me.

My brother says
He wants a rat
But they're too regular
I still want a bat!

They want to choose
A dog, cat or rat
What I don't understand
What's wrong with a bat?

Carolyn Robinson (11)
Linn Primary School

Limerick

There once was a girl from France
She loved to eat red ants
She drank some wine
In the nick of time
And ants were in her pants.

Heather Preshaw (10)
Linn Primary School

The Noisy Dog

In the house beside mine,
Lives a very noisy dog.
He barks all day long
And chases my cat, Mog!

I can't read or play
With his constant *bark, bark*
At night, I can't sleep
For his howling in the dark.

Well, I was walking home
By the lakeside one day
When I tripped and fell in
And began to float away . . .

But, the noisy dog saw me
And came racing down
He dived straight in
So I didn't drown!

Now, I can't really moan
At the noisy dog's bark
Though I love the *peace and quiet*
When he goes out to the park!

Kim Hamilton (10)
Linn Primary School

Limerick

There once was an alien from Rome
Who fell in a bucket of foam
So it went to the shower
That was in the Eiffel Tower
But it drowned and never came home.

David Murray (10)
Linn Primary School

My Granny

My granny played for Ireland,
Her name is Bet,
She kicked the ball
It deflected off the wall
And it went straight in the net!

My granny played for England,
She banged her head one day,
She got a red card
'Cause she tackled very hard
And she wasn't allowed to play!

My granny played for Wales,
She nearly scored a goal,
She ran with strides
Right up the side
And she fell into a hole!

My granny played for Scotland,
She drank too much beer,
Her bones were cracked
So she was sacked
And she ended her career.

Brandon Wilson (10)
Linn Primary School

Sky

The sky is bright
The sky is clear
It's sometimes dark
And I fill with fear
The sky has a lovely sun
In the summer
Having fun.

Shelley Barclay (9)
Portrush Primary School

My Friends

I have a friend called James,
Who is a football maniac,
He supports Man U,
I think his brain has a crack.

I have a friend called Peter,
He is my peer,
He really loves tools,
He's a born engineer.

I have a friend called Eddy,
Who has a cousin called Roy,
Eddy loves his teddy,
He's a total Mummy's boy.

I have a friend called Shelley,
Who drew a lovely poster,
She ate loads of jelly
And went on a roller coaster.

I have a friend called Sophie,
Who is good at reading,
She won a big, big trophy
And she is always leading.

I have a friend called Jane,
Who has a single pet,
She doesn't like the rain,
But she's always getting wet.

I will stick with them round all the bends
And if we split they will always be my friends.

Scott Graham (10)
Portrush Primary School

Life In A War

It is a matter of life and death,
Now that the general is dead.

Private Jones is wounded,
Correction, he is dead.

We were swearing and cursing and killing
Just for people to be free,

My brother got shot in the knee,
But the Nazis missed me!

Aaron Kane (11)
Portrush Primary School

Here's My Poem

Here's my poem so you'd better be quiet and sit.
Here's my poem so you'd better like it.
Here's my poem so you'd better listen.
It isn't about animals, school or kissin'.
Here's my poem so you'd better say that it's good,
It isn't funny, stupid or rude.
Don't look at theirs, hers or his,
Oh no! I don't know where my poem is!

Amber Callaghan (10)
Portrush Primary School

Turkey

There was a farmer called Mr Jerky
Who had a turkey
The turkey was really fat
Because it ate a cat
On Christmas Eve the turkey ran
And the next day he got fried in a pan.

James Moore (10)
Portrush Primary School

My Bed

Here I am asleep in my bed
Resting my head
With my cuddly ted.

Here I am asleep in my bed
No way am I dead
I have nothing to dread.

Here I am asleep in my bed
I'm getting close to waking
I'm feeling a strange rumbling sound
So now I know I'm quaking.

So now here I am awake like no fool
And I'm on my way, ready for school.

Matthew Quinn (10)
Portrush Primary School

A Witch That Lives In A Forest

I know a witch
That lives in a forest
And has a black cat
That drives her mad, dancing around a
Black cauldron, as the black cat
Goes after a rat that
Goes under a mat, the witch is making
Spells if you get in her way
She will turn you into a frog and
Eat you for her tea.

Rachel Pollock (10)
Portrush Primary School

Movies

I love movies
From the cinema I like best
Sinbad and Brother Bear
The Great Wild West.

Piglet's Big Movie and Lord of the Rings
The Lizzie Maguire Movie
School of Rock has a group that sings.

The big, big movie on Saturday night
Jeepers Creepers and Scary Movie
Are all full of fright.

And that's the end of my list for you
I enjoyed these
I hope you do too!

Eleanor McCollum (10)
Portrush Primary School

The New Puppy

I got a new puppy
It is six months old
And very small
When it is six years old
It will be very tall.

One day when we went to the football game
We came home and the house was ruined
The dog was sitting there
Smile on his face
Tail in the air
That is our new puppy
Now we have to redecorate.

Rose Anne Hollywood (11)
Portrush Primary School

Teachers And Kids!

Teachers go to Jupiter to get more stupider,
Kids go to Mars to get more stars!
Teachers go to space to learn to tie their lace,
Kids go to the haunted place.
Teachers get scarier,
The teachers get hairier.
Kids get older and teachers get mouldier.

Lisa-Arlene Martin (11)
Portrush Primary School

Fireworks

Fun, blasting, bursting flames
That burst upon the sky
Then drop and reflect upon my bright blue eyes.
Fireworks that bang, bash and burn
Then make a magnificent turn
They twist and twirl like a curl
Then fall onto the ground.

Megan Lennox (10)
Portrush Primary School

Night

At night I lie in my bed
Resting my sleepy head
I look out of my window to the dark
The pumping of my heart
It was faster than it's ever been
I was so scared
Of what I had seen.

Shelley Barclay (9)
Portrush Primary School

The Quite Amazing Coin

I was walking on a lovely day
When I crossed a shiny coin,
I picked it up and dropped it
And it cried out as it boinged,
'Don't catch me, don't catch me,
I don't want to be spent.'
But I put it in my pocket
And it bounced round as I went.
It spun and swirled,
Jumped and curled,
Screamed out like in pain,
'Let me go, let me go
Or I'll suck out all your brains.'
At this I was amazed
Dazzled and quite dazed,
At this tiny, little coin
Could do more than just go *boing!*
I decided it to be wise,
To let it go and not meet eyes
To keep it all the same,
Would be terribly insane!

Emma Lyons (10)
Portrush Primary School

Summer

S ummer is the best season of the year
U p and down the beach till you get to the pier.
M aking big sandcastles and digging in the sand.
M arvellous concerts with the best band.
E veryday it's sunny and bright.
R eally cold ice cream that just tastes right.

Rebekah Drennan (9)
Portrush Primary School

Feelings

When I was in Malta,
I was happy as a star.
When I was in the dirt,
I was sad and hurt.
When I was in bed and scared,
I was as lonely as a bear.
When I was sick,
I was down as a pig.
When I was a baby,
I was as scared as a lonely lady.
When I was in school,
I was as bored as a bird.

Sarah Farley (11)
Portrush Primary School

Wintertime Is Here

W is for the white snow
 I is for ice skating
N is for noses, red as can be
T is for trees green as ever
E is for everyone playing in the snow
R is for Rudolph, Christmas time.

Wintertime is here.

Elisha Kidd (10)
Rathcoole Primary School

Frostbite

W is for woolly hats
 I is for in the snow
N is for noses very sore
T is for trees with snow
E is for everybody playing snowball fights
R is for robins in the winter sky.

James Hollywood (9)
Rathcoole Primary School

Winter Wonderland

Goosebumps
Toasted flumps
People sneeze
Fingers freeze.

Snowflakes
Frozen lakes
Ice skating
People waiting.

Robins fly
Blue sky
Black ice
I've fallen twice.

Faces red
Stay in bed
Frozen toes
The colour of a rose.

White mountains
Frozen fountains
Playing in snow
Here we go!

Natasha McQuade (10)
Rathcoole Primary School

Winter Land

W inter is white as snow.
 I ce is melting too.
N oisy children shout having a snow fight.
 T he snow is glistening down the windowpane.
E verywhere is white the city lights are bright.
R unny eyes and nose you have got the cold.

Atchoo!

Andrew Lee (9)
Rathcoole Primary School

Eagles

An eagle is a bird of prey,
It kills other birds,
It goes down cliffs like a rocket,
It has claws to kill and wings to fly.

It has a mouth to eat,
It's the king of all the birds,
It's the biggest bird,
Better than all the rest!

I love the eagle's claws and jaws,
I love the eagle's wings,
I love the eagle best of all,
Because it flies above them all!

Craig Hunter (9)
Rathcoole Primary School

Fun In Winter

Winter winds.
Warm clothes.
Woolly scarf.
Husky rides.
Snowball fights.
Frosty fingers.
Icy toes.
Cold snow winter feet!

Frosty days
Stay in bed
Rest your head
Watch TV night and day
Frosty patterns, windowpanes.

Kurt Glendinning (10)
Rathcoole Primary School

Swimming Today

I hear laughing, splashing, banging everywhere
It's time to start.
'Ready? Jump in! Hurry up Declan
You'll feel warmer when you're in.'

I hate it when the water's cold
Icy showers, freezing pool
I get in slowly, but it's still polar.

I like to try to swim
Just a wee bit further than last week
Every week a wee bit more.

Clutching the red float
I think I'm going to fall in.
Swimming up to the green rope
The water is up to my shoulders.

I like swimming, it's *fun!*

Declan McCann McGreevy (11)
St Colman's Primary School, Lambeg

The Beach

The golden sand along the shore,
A large puddle of turquoise water,
Where fish live.

On the horizon natives dwell,
Some animals come out at night,
They dance beneath the stars,
Such a lovely sight.

I will never forget that night,
By the sea in the moonlight.

Niamh McGlade (11)
St Colman's Primary School, Lambeg

Witch's Spell For Riches

Boil the turkey
Make it murky
Rhino's horn
It's just born
Hedgehog spines
And some limes
Snail's shell
Cow's bell
Dog's ear
Now it can't hear
Magpie's beak
Take a peek
Bat's blood
Now it looks like mud
Drink and drink until you drop
When you wake you'll hear a pop
Then you'll be -
As rich as me!

Brian Hamill (9)
St Colman's Primary School, Lambeg

Rainbow

Red, yellow, green and blue,
Indigo, orange, violet too.
All these colours meet in the sky,
You will see them by and by.

These colours come together,
Cheer you up after dreary weather.
All of them are wonderful hues,
We like them, do you?

Catherine McCullagh (11)
St Colman's Primary School, Lambeg

Patiently Waiting

'John, get up.'
PS2 sits there waiting
'John - breakfast.'
I play for a little while
'John, you'll miss the bus.'
I leave Vice City
Breakfast, bus, school.
PS2 sits there waiting.
'Are you back? Are you coming out to play?'
PS2 sits there waiting
'John, it's time for tea.'
Now I can play,
FIFA 2004,
Vice City,
The Italian Job.
Bedtime, I dream of Grand Theft Auto.
'John, get up.'
PS2 sits there waiting.

John Connolly (11)
St Colman's Primary School, Lambeg

Rainbows In A Winter Sky

W indy days and nights
 I cicles claw on tightly to the window sills
N asty frostbites on my fingers
T rees shiver in their bareness
E xcited children playing in the snow
R ainbows light up the grey, winter sky.

Ryan Grimley (10)
St Colman's Primary School, Lambeg

Dolphin

D iving into the water
O ften splashes with its tail
L ikes to eat fish
P lays with the baby dolphins
H ates sharks killing them
I ts skin is slippy
N aughty sometimes.

Aisling McMahon (8)
St Colman's Primary School, Lambeg

Eaten In The End

G reat long neck
I t
R uns
A way
F rom
F ierce lions
E aten in the end.

Aaron Elmore (7)
St Colman's Primary School, Lambeg

Cheetah

C hases
H is
E nemy
E ats him
T ears him
A ll up
H as a nap.

Anthony Nesbitt (8)
St Colman's Primary School, Lambeg

Windy Days And Frosty Nights

W indy days and frosty nights
 I ce cold mornings
N ights are cold as ice
T oes and cheeks are as cold as icebergs
E verlasting icicles
R inkly as a frosty tree.

Conor Stephenson (11)
St Colman's Primary School, Lambeg

Giant Of Africa

G iant of Africa
 I t
R uns
A cross
F ields
F orests
E ating leaves.

Michaela Finlay (8)
St Colman's Primary School, Lambeg

Snake Attack

S lides along slowly
N estles in the grass
A ttacks with a hiss
K ill its prey
E scapes to the jungle.

Tony Fitzsimmons (10)
St Colman's Primary School, Lambeg

Leaves In Autumn

Crushing leaves with my hand
Leaves twisting round and round
Floating, floating to the ground.

James Henderson (8)
St Colman's Primary School, Lambeg

Monster

Monster, oh monster, so ugly and fat
Monster, oh monster, watch out there under the mat
Monster, oh monster, their scheming is evil
Monster, oh monster, they will render you feeble
Monster, oh monster, they're mangy and mean
Monster, oh monster, this is not a dream
Monster, oh monster, they're muttering under their breath
Monster, oh monster, they'll scare you to death.

Ciarán Crossan (11)
St Joseph's Primary School, Crumlin

I Thought

When I heard about mystical, magical places,
I thought I'd adventure and meet new faces.
I thought that I'd meet an evil snow queen,
I thought I'd see stuff that no one has seen.
I thought I'd ride with unicorns and horses,
I thought I'd race around race track courses.
But now that I'm older I'm starting to realise,
That being with your family takes first prize.

Emma Louise Friel (10)
St Joseph's Primary School, Crumlin

Dreams

Today was a pretty normal day.
I walked to school in a normal way,
I went outside at lunch to play
But it all changed . . .

I fell asleep in my normal bed
Dreams running through my head
Huddled in blankets and blue and red
But I woke up . . .

I heard a noise outside my room
Noises rumbling through the gloom
It all just ended with an almighty *boom!*
Silence now.

I opened up my bedroom door
My bare feet padding along the floor
But then I heard a deafening roar
From the living room.

The door led into a different place
Somewhere in the middle of outer space
In front of me I saw the ugliest face
An alien.

Its tentacles stretched far and wide
A transparent creature with green blood inside
It was so scary I could have cried
But it vanished.

I jumped up with a terrified shout
What was that dream all about?
What's going on, the light's not out?
It was all just a dream
Wasn't it?

Jennifer Mackel (10)
St Joseph's Primary School, Crumlin

Homework, I Hate You

Homework, oh homework
I hate you, you stink
You make me work
You make me think.

Homework, oh homework
I hate you
I do
I wish I could flush you down the loo.

There's nothing about homework
I actually like
When my teacher says, 'Take down your homework,'
I feel like saying, *'Take a hike!'*

But when I get home
At my door I feel like collapsing, I do
I have to do the dreaded homework
I wanted to flush down the loo.

Rory McKeown (10)
St Joseph's Primary School, Crumlin

My Dog

My dog is called Spot
And he eats a lot.
He is very lazy
And when he is sick he gets very dazy.
My dog is called Spot
And he eats a lot.
He likes to go for a walk
And I wish he could talk.
This is what my dog is like,
But be warned, he has a nasty bite.

Alicia Connolly (11)
St Joseph's Primary School, Crumlin

My Dog

My dog is grey, white and black,
She jumps all over your back,
She lies at the door,
You even hear her snore,
At the front door and back.

When the door is open,
She just shoots out,
She just goes out and runs about,
When we go to catch her,
She runs away,
All she wants to do is play.

Kathryn Bawn (11)
St Joseph's Primary School, Crumlin

My Mummy

My mummy is the best mum ever,
She really is whatever the weather.
She is so nice and so kind,
She makes me happy when she comes to mind.
I really love her with all my heart
And I really hope we'll never part.
My mum always stands out in a crowd,
Because she does it makes me proud.
My mum buys me whatever I need
And I never, ever have to plead.
I really, really love her so,
I hope this will get published then she will know!

Kathryn Edwards (11)
St Joseph's Primary School, Crumlin

Homework

Homework, I hate you,
Homework, you darken my day,
But homework will never go away.
Maths, English, science,
Every day.
You are dull, full of annoyance,
From nine times nine to
What is buoyant.
I can't help wanting to rip you up
And flush you down the toilet.
You are one of life's down points,
Lowest of low.
Why can't you just disappear,
But it's not as simple as that,
Oh no,
I want my own back.

Peter McAlernon (11)
St Joseph's Primary School, Crumlin

My Own Country

My own country is Ireland,
The North I am from.
From the rioting in Belfast,
To the bombing of Omagh.
The South is quiet,
Full of verdant grass.
With trees and lakes
And attractive beaches too.
But I think the North is best,
With plenty of things to do.

Thomas Wallace Bigger (11)
St Joseph's Primary School, Crumlin

Gymnastics

Gymnasts can take the pain,
But we suffer hours of strain.
Here we twist and twirl,
We also jump and whirl.

Heather Mallon (10)
St Joseph's Primary School, Crumlin

Pickles

I love Pickles fat and round.
My love for Pickles knows no bounds.
When I get home, I have Pickles on my lap,
By the way, Pickles is my cat!

Suzi Ernst (11)
St Joseph's Primary School, Crumlin

Crossing The Road

Fire-breathing dragons
Really make me shiver.
Monsters coming at me
One after the other.
First from my left,
Then from my right.
I put one foot forward,
Peering from side to side.
Got to keep going.
I think I'm going to make it.
Yes!
I've crossed the road.

Ciaran McIlfatrick (9)
St Joseph's Primary School, Dunloy

ELS

(ELS - Emergency Life Support)

An accident can happen day or night.
It might even give you a little fright.
ELS is great fun.
It's even made for everyone.
We took photos, we used dummies.
We pressed on people's tummies.
Make sure you move stuff like a knife.
It might even save the person's life.
If they have a bad heart.
Make sure you know what to do from the start.
If they take a stroke.
Put them in a position that they will not boke.
If they get a bite.
Wrap it up tight.

Conor Crawford (10)
St Joseph's Primary School, Dunloy

Interesting Sounds

Wind whistling
Bacon sizzling
Tap dancing shoes
On a wooden floor
The mighty cheer
When my team score
The *zzzziiiipppp*
Of my pencil case opening
Birds singing
These are the sounds I love.

Ronan Cunning (9)
St Joseph's Primary School, Dunloy

The Deadly Hawk

A hawk has razor-sharp claws to
Guide its way into the body of
A rabbit.
Its beak to tear and swallow the
Meat.
When it is flying its eyes are like
A telescope to the ground.
Flying back to its chicks with a
Supply of meat.

Justin Drain (11)
St Joseph's Primary School, Dunloy

Magpie Robbery

Magpies steal
Shiny wheels
Someone stop them
Please.

Lots of things
Diamond rings
We've got to find them
Now!

Lauren Elliott (10)
St Joseph's Primary School, Dunloy

The Dancing Duck

When the Irish music started
His wings began to twitch
His feet began to prance
There wasn't anything he could do
So he started to dance.

Rosie McNamee (9)
St Joseph's Primary School, Dunloy

The Falcon

The falcon is quick and fierce,
With its talons it will pierce,
Right through birds' skin and feathers
To feed itself and its young.
So watch out, if the falcon meets
An unsuspecting bird, great feast!

Niall O'Boyle (11)
St Joseph's Primary School, Dunloy

The Golden Eagle

A golden eagle in flight
Is a wondrous sight,
It's soaring above,
Scanning the ground.
Suddenly it dives,
To end some hapless squirrels life.

Seamus McLaughlin (11)
St Joseph's Primary School, Dunloy

Beautiful Creatures

B is for building nests in trees
I nteresting behaviour
R earing their young
D eciding where to migrate to
S omewhere to sleep or protect their outstanding bodies.

Katherine McToal (11)
St Joseph's Primary School, Dunloy

ELS

(ELS - Emergency Life Support)

It starts off like a normal day
But you hear a shout for help while you play
You find a man who's bleeding seriously
And he gives you a scare
There's nothing to hurt you so you shout for help
But nobody's there
You don't have your mobile with you
So what do you do?
You take off your jumper and wrap it
Round his wound and he jumps with a start.
You raise his wound high above his heart.
You go to the payphone and call 999.
Then you tell what the sign says.
A minutes later the ambulance came
The man said thanks
And that some barbed wire was to blame.

Emma Dooey (11)
St Joseph's Primary School, Dunloy

My Class

Our class is a very nice place, it is very big and full of space.
We do a lot of history and sometimes we even read a story.
We can look out the window and see lots of houses and
Cars go by and then we wish we were outside too
And begin to think and cry.
In our 'Alive-o 7' we do about people in Heaven.
I sit beside Shane and I'm very happy our school doesn't have a cane.
I like our class, it is the best and better than all the rest!

Melissa Cunning (11)
St Joseph's Primary School, Dunloy

Fear

My eyes snap open.
I slip out and go
Down, down, down
Into the gloomy hall.
A door opens,
A shadow looms.
A vampire?
A voice booms,
'Get back into bed, Paul!
It's very late!'

Paul Cochrane (9)
St Joseph's Primary School, Dunloy

The Woodpecker

The woodpecker pecks on his little, hollow tree,
Pecking away busily,
When dark falls he must leave his tree
And bring back some food for his family.

Patsy Martin (10)
St Joseph's Primary School, Dunloy

Friends

Secret keepers
Tear wipers
Smile makers
Sweet buyers
Fair dealers
Fight breakers
Team makers
That's my best friends!

Ronan Shivers (9)
St Joseph's Primary School, Dunloy

High Noon

11.00 I don't want to go,
But I have to,
I don't want to die,
But I have to,
It's the fang mangler,
With fangs on his head,
Is it a zombie?
No. A witch?
Wizard?
Devil?
Ghost?
Grim Reaper?
11.30 I'm in the ante-chamber,
11.45 I see shadows looming,
12.00
It's the monster . . .
Noooooooo!
It's the dentist!

Thomas McCann (9)
St Joseph's Primary School, Dunloy

Dark Fear

Scary, black holes,
Spine-tingling, dark rooms,
Frightening, dark forests,
Dark!
Evil's all around,
Devils, bogeymen.
It's coming closer.
It's bending,
Oh! It's Mum,
Checking that I'm asleep.

Patrick Magee (9)
St Joseph's Primary School, Dunloy

I'm Glad

I'm glad when it's spring
When winter's snow goes away
And lambs come out to play.
I'm glad when it's summer
When leaves are green and flowers bright.
It seems much longer until night.
I'm glad when it's autumn
When harvest begins and leaves go brown.
I get to dress up in my witch's gown.
I'm glad when it's winter.
When we wrap up warm
To go out in the snow to play
And Santa Claus flies over on his sleigh.

Lauren McQuillan (8)
St Joseph's Primary School, Dunloy

Fear

I hate being in the dark.
I search for the light switch
But can't find it.
What's going on?
What's going to happen to me now?
Will I die or will I be swallowed up by the dark?
I take two small steps forward.
OK so far.
I haven't fallen into a black hole.
I reach out and find the switch.
The room is filled with light.
I'm not afraid anymore.

John-lee Smyth (9)
St Joseph's Primary School, Dunloy

Fear

I search for the light switch.
Oh no! It's not there.
What will happen now?
Will I be swallowed by monsters?
Will I fall into a black hole?
I put one foot forward
Then the other
OK so far.
I open the door
There's something there
What is it?
I feel hot breath on my face.
What is it?
The hairs on my neck are standing.
The light bursts on.
Oh! It's just Mammy.

Niall Doherty (8)
St Joseph's Primary School, Dunloy

Shivers

Into the noisy room I stumble
And slither into a chair
Closer, closer, closer she looms
Her sharp weapon in the air
Aiming at my neck
I take a deep breath and say,
'Just a little trim please.
It's getting quite long!'

Aimee McPoland (9)
St Joseph's Primary School, Dunloy

Fear

Being locked in,
Crossing the road,
Dark corners,
Dizzy heights.
Fear . . .
Loops on roller coasters,
Upstairs in the dark,
Hearing footsteps outside at night,
Shadows in my bedroom.
Fear!

Christy Drain (9)
St Joseph's Primary School, Dunloy

Friends

By your side,
Each step of the way.
Always there for you.
That safe feeling surrounds you.
Sharing secrets.
Listening ears.
No more tears.
Feeling important.
Exchanging presents.
That's what friends are for.

Caoimhe McCullagh (9)
St Joseph's Primary School, Dunloy

The Monster

Jaw breaker
Scream maker
Sweet checker
Fang shaper
Tooth driller
Smile shaker
Jab giver
Rot exterminator
Hole filler . . .
The dentist!

Adam O'Kane (9)
St Joseph's Primary School, Dunloy

I'm Not Scared

Tall ghosts
Short ghosts
But I'm not scared
Creepy ghosts
Scary ghosts
Ones with gleaming, red eyes.
Ones flying about you
Never knowing
Where they are
But I'm not scared.

James Kearns (8)
St Joseph's Primary School, Dunloy

Nightmare

Gloomy shadows
Creeping in the dark
Evil red eyes
Sharp pointed fangs
Shiny black horns
I look for a light
In the dark of night
I see those eyes
They make me shiver
Why did I choose
Such a scary book
To read at bedtime!

Sean Hurl (9)
St Joseph's Primary School, Dunloy

Ah! This Is The Life!

Watching Neighbours when homework's done,
Home alone with my music on *loud!*
Soaking in a hot bath,
Snuggled deeply in my bed,
The tingling sensation
Of the first bite of chocolate,
Lying on a towel at the beach,
At a sleepover with my friends,
That's my idea of *Heaven!*

Olivia McLaughlin (9)
St Joseph's Primary School, Dunloy

The Mummy

It's coming up the stairs
Thump, thump thump
It's nearly here . . .
I scramble into my room
I can't get to sleep
It keeps me awake
Coming closer, closer
My heart's thumping
Phew!
It's only my mum
Checking if I'm asleep.

Ryan Reynolds (9)
St Joseph's Primary School, Dunloy

Fear

Here, there, everywhere
Fear!
They're all over me
Fear!
I hate them. I really do.
Guess what it is?
My biggest fear is this . . .
Big, small, hairy or smooth
I hate them!
Creepy, creepy, creepy.
Spinning webs,
Aaaaargh . . .
Spiders!

Nichola Cassidy (9)
St Joseph's Primary School, Dunloy

The Two-Eyed Monster

Oh no!
My life's nearly over.
Here it comes.
What is it?
Is it a bogeyman?
Or is it a vampire?
I don't know
I go into a deep, dark room
He sets a heavy blindfold on my nose
A voice booms, 'What can you see?'
Aaah! Oooh! Wwwhy! Mmmm!
It's . . . It's . . .
The optician.

Sorcha Doherty (8)
St Joseph's Primary School, Dunloy

In The Corner Of My Room

It's terrifying!
I often wonder
What lies in the corner?
There could be a monster
Or a skeleton.
I would never dare to look
Into the corner of my room.
Then I realise
There's no such thing as ghosts.

Daren Cunning (9)
St Joseph's Primary School, Dunloy

Heights

I tremble all over
Looking down with a shiver
I feel like I'm going to fall
Into the river.

Knees knocking
Against each other.
Teeth chattering up and down.
Stomach rumbles with an ache.
Get me down from here
For goodness sake!

James McFall (8)
St Joseph's Primary School, Dunloy

Feeling Sad

Rushing home at 3 o'clock
To be first on the computer.
My brother dances with rage.
He punches me, I howl
And punch him back.
Dad puts the computer off,
'Homework first!' he roars.
We hang our heads in shame.
I can't rush because Dad will check.
I could be here all night.

Kevin Armstrong (8)
St Joseph's Primary School, Dunloy

Bed Bugs

Help . . .
They're coming to get me.
They're crawling up my back.
With their long, black legs.
Oh, now they're on my head
Now they are on my face
I must be nearly dead
They really make me shiver,
Turn, twist and quiver in my bed.

Niamh McAuley (9)
St Joseph's Primary School, Dunloy

Dogs

Their big, sharp claws
As sharp as can be,
Their big jaws open up at me.
Dogs
If I make one move,
They'll just jump on me
Rip me to bits
And eat me for tea.

Conor Taylor (8)
St Joseph's Primary School, Dunloy

The She-Devil

Watch out!
There's a devil about.
She gobbles mobile phones
And scares me with a mask.
She tortures little sisters
And screams at little brothers.
If you see her coming . . . *run!*
She's my big sister.

Michael Rodgers (9)
St Joseph's Primary School, Dunloy

A Winter's Day

On a freezing winter's day
I am in bed, I can't go
I have the cold, I want to play
But it's too cold on this winter's day.
I am in bed, stuck
I have to take medicine, *yuck!*

My cold is away now,
I can go out to play.
I've made a snowman on this winter's day.
I play a snowball fight -
Then the snow melts away!

Megan McAllister (7)
St MacNissi's Primary School, Larne

The Goblin's Cellar

Alone, the goblin sat in the deep, dark, fusty cellar,
As the dark night fell,
The moon lit up the sky,
Casting a shadow into the mouldy, dreary cellar,
In the corner, two eyes glistened,
Forever watchful for its prey,
The slimy creature lurked,
Motionless in its domain,
Only bones remained,
Of those that had gone before us,
In this perilous place!

Emily Campbell (9)
St MacNissi's Primary School, Larne

My Mummy

My mummy is as sweet as honey,
She wears a bikini when it is sunny,
When she gets brown she turns around,
But when winter comes she's like a bear,
She stays indoors in case she gets froze.
But when the sun comes back out she goes
To pick up where she left off.
I think she's like a rose.

So Mum, this is for you!
Mum this is a poem for you
You're the very best by far.
You're extra nice and extra fun
It's the way you always are.
Times are fun when you're around
No nicer mum could ever be found.
You're the greatest kind of mum
Any child has ever had!
Love you Mum!

AmyLeigh McMullan (9)
Star Of The Sea Primary School

What Colour!

What is red?
A rose is red, growing in my garden shed.

What is blue?
The sky is blue, that's the one birds go through.

What is pink?
A flower is pink, that's the colour that makes the boys wink.

What is white?
A horse is white, cantering through the moonlight.

What is yellow?
The Simpsons are yellow, a happy, funny little fellow.

Cailin Millar (9)
Star Of The Sea Primary School

The Coming Of Spring

Everywhere you look around,
Snow is melting on the ground
The birds are flapping wild about
As if they know the sun is coming out.

There is a crispness in the air
Making people look and stare
At the grass shoots growing
In the ground where it was once bare.

All the flowers are sprouting out
Now that spring is coming about
Even the children are running wild about
Making a lot of noise and beginning to shout.

Out comes their games from far away
So that they can begin to play
Hip! Hip! Hooray!
Spring is here to *stay!*

Nadine McNally (10)
Star Of The Sea Primary School

The Sickle In The Sky

She dances,
In splendour,
Her clarified essence lighting up the bleak night sky.
Oh Silvery Goddess!
Thou hast guided me from birth -
And now mine eyes are opened!
For once I thought thee evil, gibbous, satanic.
But now, oh queen of the night -
I see your true aura!
Pure, shimmering, bewitching - lo!
You light the night,
For our delight,
Till the sun shouldst call the day.

Cáragh Cassidy (10)
Star Of The Sea Primary School

If I Owned A Sweet Shop

If I owned a sweet shop
Every sweet would be there
If I owned a fruit shop
Nobody would care.

If I owned a chip shop
The chips wouldn't be small
If I owned a toy shop
I'd have them all.

If I owned a furniture shop
I'd have every piece there is
If I owned a clothes shop
I would be the new bizz.

If I owned a curtain shop
The curtains would be made of wool
If I owned a tool shop
Everyone would want tools.

Although I like all these things, I have to decide
It will take long, so I think I'll have a seat
I think I'll try a sweet shop
Because I like sweets.

Melissa McCabe (9)
Star Of The Sea Primary School

My Best Friend, Lauren

Lauren and I have been friends since we were two
She is kind and warm and lots of fun too.

We are always together with lots to do,
She make me laugh night and day too.

Lauren is like the sunshine she brightens up my day
And if I'm feeling sad she knows just what to say.

Ciara McShane (9)
Star Of The Sea Primary School

A Watering Rhyme

Early in the morning
Or the evening hour
Are the times to water
Every kind of flower
Watering at noonday
When the sun is high
Doesn't help the flowers
Only makes them die
Also when you water
Water at the roots
Flowers keep their mouths there
We would wear our boots
Soak the earth around them
Then through all the heat
The flowers will have water
For their thirsty feet.

Orla McLaughlin (8)
Star Of The Sea Primary School

My Teddy

I love my teddy
My teddy is brown
He wears a crown
When I cuddle him at night
He sometimes gets a fright
When he gets in the pool
He thinks he is cool
He is a big bear
He has lots of hair
And he doesn't really care
I love my teddy
And he loves me.

Shannon McWilliams (9)
Star Of The Sea Primary School

Seasons

Spring is full of sun
New creatures are being born
Buds are starting to grow on trees
Daffodils are opening up
Time to put light clothes on
Air is getting warmer.

Summer is full of sun
Sometimes rainy but mostly sunny
People are going on holidays
Some people staying at home
Getting tan everywhere
Summer has to make way for autumn.

Autumn is full of rain
Leaves are falling from trees
People are putting on warmer clothes
Creatures are growing big
The air is getting colder
It is coming into winter.

Winter is here now
Snow is falling down
People are wearing very warm clothes
It is nearly Christmas
People are getting excited
Now it is going back to spring.

Aisling Kerr (9)
Star Of The Sea Primary School

September (Skipping Rhyme)

Back to school
Back to school
Mustn't be late
Eat toast
Leave the house
Half-past eight.

Back to school
Back to school
We feel sad
Wintertime
Been and here again
Yes, I'm glad.

Here we are
Out of school
Playing with my friends
Street games
Into bed
School ends.

Aimee McKiernan (10)
Star Of The Sea Primary School

Nature's Miracles

Nested in the darkness
Well beneath the snow.
Something wonderful is happening.
Just starting to grow.
The weather soon will change to bright
A little bud will show its head
And reach up to the light.
The garden will burst with colour
A wonderful sight to see
Mother Nature's miracle
Just for you and me.

Megan Curley (9)
Star Of The Sea Primary School

I Love Everyone

I love my mummy
She is sweeter
Than honey.

I love my dad
Even when
He is sad.

I love my sister
The boy next door
Kissed her.

I love my gran
She is a big
Celtic fan.

I love my aunties
They wear
Frilly panties.

I love my uncle
He has
A carbuncle.

I love everyone
It is not hard
To be done.

Seanain Mahon (9)
Star Of The Sea Primary School

Starvation

When I see children on TV
It makes me feel so sad deep inside,
Because they remind me of when I have no food in my belly.
When we watch these children on telly.
When I see these people of different nations on TV
Because of starvation I would like to be able to help
And give food for their nation.
When we see them on telly,
If the government of their country had all the means and equipment,
It's only a taste of water.
Then the country would start to generate
And we would ask each other
What is the matter with our world.

Émer Kelly (8)
Star Of The Sea Primary School

Colours

What is red?
Roses are red, as red as the blood in my veins.
What is blue?
The sky is blue, as blue as the ocean deep.
What is brown?
Chocolate is brown, as brown as my lovely long hair.
What is yellow?
The sun is yellow, as yellow as a fresh banana.
What is pink?
Candyfloss is pink, as pink as my soft, rosy cheeks.
What is green?
Grass is green, as green as the leaves on the trees.

Natasha O'Hare (9)
Star Of The Sea Primary School

About Me

My name is Casey, I am nine years old
I always do what I am told.
I am tall and thin with beautiful hair
And if you see me you would say I am fair.

I have three sisters and a little cat,
My mummy says it looks like a rat.
I love to play everyday
And then on Friday I get my pay.

When I grow up I want to be,
Just as beautiful as can be.
Because I know that every day,
God loves me in a special way.

Casey-Leigh Hillick (9)
Star Of The Sea Primary School

My Favourite Smells

The smell of mixed nuts in the pet shop,
I love the smell of melted chocolate,
Sitting in the car, sniffing the fumes of petrol,
Smearing little black dress perfume on myself,
The smell of grass that's just been cut,
The smell of the dentist's gloves,
I love the smell of food in the car,
The smell of my strawberry lipbalm.

Bryony Chapman (9)
Woodburn Primary School

I Love You Though . . .

I love you though it feels like you're going to stop,
I love you though your doors are about to come off,
I love you though your exhaust rattles on the road,
I love you though your engine has nearly exploded,
I love you though your lights don't have full beam,
I love you though your steering wheel is half on and half off,
I love you though your seats are torn off,
I love you though you have no seats,
I love you, toy car.

Adam Moore (9)
Woodburn Primary School

Listen, Can You Hear?

The wind in Stephen's car on Saturday,
My mum closing her bedroom door,
The teacher laughing,
A car starting up,
The lunch bell ringing,
My PlayStation getting going,
The classroom door slamming.

Samuel Stewart (9)
Woodburn Primary School

How To Make An Elephant . . .

A trunk like a tree trunk,
A body like a blown up balloon,
Eyes like small, black balls,
Feet like big, round, shiny, flat stones,
Ears like big, round lumps of freshly cut grass,
A tail like fluffy string,
A head like a big, shiny, golden ball.

Corrie Johnston (9)
Woodburn Primary School

The Storm, Like An Orchestra

The storm is like an orchestra
Screaming wind flying through the air
Like a high-pitched flute
Crashing waves plundering the waters
Like thrashing cymbals
Hailstones clattering from the skies
Like a low-pitched piano note
Frightening thunder clashing down from the sky
Like banging bass drums
Mystical black sky
Like a war tune played on a trumpet
Gleaming lightning flashing up above
Like a storm tuned harp
Translucent fog calming the air
Like a cello playing softly
Now the storm is calming
As if it never existed.

Matthew Crawford (11)
Woodburn Primary School